THE CAPTAIN

A Story About REAL Leadership

Jamy Bechler
Author of *The Bus Trip*

Copyright © 2021 by Jamy Bechler
www.JamyBechler.com

All rights reserved. No part of this publication may be reproduced, stored in a retrieval system, or transmitted, in any form or by any means, electronic, mechanical, photocopying, recording, or otherwise, without the prior written permission of the author, except in the case of brief quotations embodied in critical reviews and certain other noncommercial uses permitted by copyright law.

This book contains information obtained from authentic and highly regarded sources. Reasonable efforts have been made to publish reliable data and information, but the author and publisher cannot assume responsibility for the validity of all materials or the consequences of their use.

ISBN: 978-0-9992125-8-5

Team or bulk orders are available by contacting
support@mhbookservices.com

Online programs for leadership and team captains are offered at
TheLeadershipPlaybook.com

Chapter discussion guides for this book can be found at
JamyBechler.com/TheCaptainBook

The Captain is a work of fiction designed to help individuals understand how to be better teammates and more positive leaders. Names, characters, businesses, organizations, places, events, incidents, or locales are the product of the author's imagination or are used fictitiously. Any resemblance to actual persons, living or dead, or locales is entirely coincidental.

THANK YOU …

Tristen Foote for organizing and leading our book launch team. You've been invaluable throughout this process, and we couldn't have done it without you.

Our launch team members for spreading the word about the book.

Andy "Grand" Mariner for all the time you spent as military consultant for the book. Your experience as a U.S. Navy captain and TOPGUN commanding officer was crucial to my writing. Though the book probably isn't perfect in every single detail, we tried to be as true to the spirit of Naval aviation as possible. This book would not have been possible without your help with context and storylines.

To my parents, Frank and Beth Bechler, for providing me an example of how to be a person of influence when holding a leadership position. It was never about the title for them. It was always about making things better for the world around them.

Mathoni Villegas for the cover design.

MH Book Services for editing, formatting, and producing the book.

Deion "Coach Prime" Sanders, Pat Fitzgerald, and Adrian Griffin for the back-cover book endorsement.

My son Jaylen who begged me to be included in my new book even though he's yet to read any of my other ones. Maybe when I write one about eSports and a professional gamer, he'll read it cover-to-cover. Regardless, thank you Jaylen for letting daddy pound away on his keyboard on those days he absolutely needed to. Daddy loves Jaylen!

My last (but certainly not least) "thank you" goes out to Tabitha for your love, support, and encouragement throughout this process. This book would not have been possible without you. I love you.

This book is dedicated to all the men and women that have served in the military. Freedom isn't free and we appreciate the sacrifices each individual (and their family) has made to keep us safe.

CONTENTS

1. Mayday 1
2. Omaha 2
3. Maverick 3
4. Successful Audible 4
5. Punching Out 5
6. Football Press Conference 6
7. Floating to Earth 8
8. Post-Game Talk 10
9. Cell Phone 12
10. Recruiting Letter 13
11. Letter from TOPGUN 16
12. Alone with his Thoughts 18
13. Offensive Lineman 19
14. Parachute Landing 21
15. Talking with Backup 23
16. Status Report 26
17. Injury 27
18. Rescue Plan 29
19. At the Hospital 30
20. Great Teammates 32
21. Flight Suit 36
22. Team Travel Suit 38
23. Jackie Robinson 42
24. Weather Gets Bad 45
25. Snowy Football Game 47
26. Delayed Rescue 50

CONTENTS

27. Heisman Winner 52
28. Rescue Team is a Go 54
29. Brady's Rescue 55
30. Ex-Backup in the NFL 57
31. Taking Responsibility 60
32. Helicopter Takes Off 63
33. Sequoia Hospital 64
34. The Doctor 65
35. White Christmas 68
36. Guard Dog 71
37. Heavy Lifting 73
38. Leaving the Hospital 76
39. Philly Special 78
40. Back on Base 81
41. Meeting with Grand 84
42. Redwood Trees 86
43. Coach Casey Honored 90
44. Review Board 95
45. Brady's Request 98
46. Surprise Letter 102
47. Letter to Coach Casey 105
48. Responsible for the Team 106
49. Empower Others 108
50. Able to Connect 110
51. Lead by Example 112
52. Real Leaders 114

MAYDAY

"Mayday! Mayday! Mayday!"
"Engine shutdown. I'm going down. Mayday! Mayday! Mayday! Maverick 2-2-9. I'm punching out. Over."

As he completed the message, Captain Brady Thomas ejected from his FA-18 Hornet somewhere over the Sierra Mountain range on his latest "routine" training run.

OMAHA

"Mayday! Mayday! Mayday!"

Despite the deafening roar from the 80,000 screaming fans, these words from the quarterback were loud and clear to the offensive players that the defense was about to blitz.

The called play was in trouble.

The game clock was counting down 1:15, 1:14, 1:13, 1:12...

He'd seen the great Peyton Manning use his "Omaha" audible countless times, and now Brady Thomas would use his own "Mayday" call. The quarterback audibled into the anti-blitz play.

He took a quick glance back at his tailback and then checked out the strong safety position once more.

Even though the defense knew what play the offense was running, the star quarterback was cool, calm, and collected as his instincts and training took over.

Plus, he knew something the defense didn't know.

He'd just changed the play.

"Mayday! Mayday! Mayday! Red 23. Hut. Hut!"

MAVERICK

Brady had flown over the Sierras hundreds of times, but this was the first time he'd wished he'd paid more attention to the terrain and the nuances of the mountain range.

Though he'd trained for this kind of situation, he'd never punched out during his decorated Naval aviation career.

"Maverick" was about to find out what it felt like in a real-life emergency.

Brady loved the movie *Top Gun,* but the call sign was given to him by his peers. It was not a term of affection. He considered himself confident and accomplished. His peers thought of him as overrated and cocky.

Regardless, the Senior Officers thought it was funny when Brady was given the moniker as a Junior Officer. He knew it was a rite of passage. He knew he wouldn't always be a Junior Officer, so he couldn't let them know it bothered him.

Brady was well-trained and in mere seconds, calmly went through all his emergency protocols.

Despite his composed demeanor, there was no time to reminisce about his early days as a J.O. or his accomplishments or his fast-tracked promotions as one of the Navy's youngest Captains.

However, he did allow one unproductive thought to creep into his mind. How could this be happening to him, of all people?

SUCCESSFUL AUDIBLE

Immediately upon hearing the second "hut" from his quarterback's mouth, the center snapped the ball.

Brady turned to his left to handoff the ball to the tailback, but the strong safety immediately shot the gap, tackling the running back in what appeared to be a huge loss of yards.

But Brady had faked the handoff.

He was now rolling out to his right on a bootleg, quickly throwing to the tight end cutting across the middle of the field exactly where the strong safety would have been if he hadn't blitzed.

It was a perfectly executed play, and the tight end would not be caught as he sprinted 55 yards to the endzone, sealing the victory for State.

The crowd was finally silenced, but Brady and his teammates were making enough noise for everyone.

Millions of football fans across the country were enamored by State's freshman phenom. Brady Thomas had taken the nation by storm and was already being considered as a potential All-American even though the season had barely reached the halfway point.

PUNCHING OUT

Captain Brady Thomas needed perfect execution now in this life-or-death situation.

He pulled the ejection handle.

The cockpit canopy immediately detached from the fighter jet.

The Naval aviator was shot up into the air.

The chute deployed.

Brady was now safely gliding back down to earth.

He was going to be okay, which couldn't be said for his jet.

Brady watched the $70 million jet crash into the rocky terrain.

It was frustrating that he couldn't find a way to keep the plane airborne.

Even after losing power, it was a shame that he couldn't find a piece of flat land and just glide the jet down for an emergency landing as seen on TV or in the movies.

These FA-18s did not operate like that. Once they lost power, they essentially dropped like a rock. A 34-ton rock. Fortunately, modern technology made these ejection seats zero altitude meaning a pilot could punch out at any point before the plane crashed. Brady had tried to get it flying again, waiting until the last possible moment to punch out.

The Navy didn't recommend cutting it so close, but "Maverick" had plenty of practice playing it close to the edge from his football glory days.

FOOTBALL PRESS CONFERENCE

The journalist from the Tribune was the first one called on by State's Sports Information Director.

"Brady, that was a well-executed play on that last touchdown. I imagine with your style of play; you love that your coaches are willing to take risks instead of playing it safe and running out the clock. What were your thoughts when the play came in?"

"Actually, we audibled," Brady responded. "The strong safety knew what play was coming. It was supposed to be a handoff, and they would have tackled us for a loss. I've seen them do that on film and figured we could capitalize on the opportunity…and that's what we did."

The reporter then asked, "I see, so your coach give you that kind of freedom?"

"I've seen Peyton Manning do his Omaha, Omaha, Omaha audible to perfection play after play, so we put in our own special audible. One of my favorite movies growing up was *Top Gun* so I figured let's substitute Mayday for Omaha since it signifies that we're in trouble. We've done it a couple of times this year but never in such a crucial situation. It was awesome seeing it work."

A reporter from the Chronicle asked a follow-up question.

"Just to clarify, you're saying Coach Casey was okay with that call at the end of the game? I understand you have that option in your playbook, but was he okay with you doing it at the end of the game like that?"

With a slight grin, Brady said, "I'm confident he is okay with it. We won, didn't we?"

State's Sports Information Director motioned in the direction of another reporter, and the questions continued for another five minutes.

As he walked back to the locker room, Brady felt like he was floating on cloud nine. After today's amazing victory, he is now the talk of the nation. He is the man. Life is great.

FLOATING TO EARTH

As he floated to earth, he was glad to be alive but hardly grateful. Instead, he was furious. What happened up there? This was a routine training run…until it wasn't.

The spectacular sunset-drenched view all around him revealed purple mountains against the blazing orange desert. But the beauty didn't register as much as the surreal feeling in his gut. Bready thought, "This is like a very vivid dream." It probably had more to do with the fact that he just couldn't believe he was in this predicament.

How could this be happening to him of all people?

His heart was still beating like a drum and adrenalin continued to course through his veins, but the world started to slow down around him. His awareness of his surroundings solidified. His training kicked in to take over the fear and anger.

This situation reminded him of playing quarterback, and how he could visualize things before they happened. He trained to be well prepared. That training combined with talent and mental toughness is why he was always successful.

His mind works differently than others.

Right now, he was glad to be okay, but he never really considered any other outcome.

He was always successful.

THE CAPTAIN

He was a four-year starter at quarterback for one of college football's elite programs and had earned the rank of "O6" in the U.S. Navy, becoming one of the youngest captains in Naval history.

He worked hard and earned what he wanted.

Success was expected. Failure was not.

This was different.

This was not expected.

How did this happen? Who screwed up?

His thoughts turned to getting rescued so he could go find the people who failed during the preflight inspection that led to his jet's malfunction.

He would get to the bottom of this.

He was always successful.

POST-GAME TALK

Coach Casey typically waited until the guys got showered and dressed before giving his post-game talk. This allowed players and coaches time to meet with the media when they were obligated to do so.

As Brady finished zipping up his travel top, the coaching staff gathered the players into the middle of the locker room.

"Okay, listen up guys. First off, congrats on the win."

Cheers, high-fives, and smiles filled the room.

"Secondly, we'll talk about this more during the film session on Monday, but that last offensive play was unnecessary. It was dangerous."

His mind seemed to be on a million different things, but Coach's comment snapped Brady back into the moment.

"We have to consider the big picture! We must see the forest and not just our own little tree. Tech had no timeouts left. Even if they tackled us for a loss, we still could have let the clock run down for a punt on 4th down. They might have even gotten the ball back, but there would've only been a few seconds left in the game. The chances they could have marched down the field to score a touchdown were slim. The clock was our friend. We just needed to let it run. Tech couldn't stop it. A score was fun, but there are a dozen scenarios that could have worked against us. That pass could have been intercepted or if we had been sacked, we would have been in serious trouble. That trouble could have translated into failure not just for this game, but also for the rest of the season if someone had gotten injured."

Brady felt like Coach Casey was lecturing him directly, which was strange. "Did he want to win games or not?" Brady thought to himself. As Coach continued his post-game talk, the words barely registered with Brady.

"This is why we talk about this in position meetings every week. We constantly review and run these different two-minute scenarios to make sure you guys are paying attention and learning. Learn to listen and listen to learn. These two-minute drills are not just about winning football games. One of these days, the lessons these coaches keep trying to engrain in your heads will pop up when you least expect it. Today, the gamble worked, but the takeaway from this win is failure."

After a couple of announcements, the team exited the stadium for the return trip to State's campus.

Coach Casey had hoped to the team's attention – in particular, Brady's attention. However, Brady was much more interested in being the focus of the media and fans once he left the locker room. Every time he saw a TV – in the airport, restaurant, store, or the dorms – it was his highlights that were being replayed.

He was a star, and he had the receipts to prove it.

Big-name athletes, media personalities, and even some celebrities were blowing up his phone. Text after text came across the screen of his cell phone. That was proof enough that he was the man.

Brady was starting to get frustrated with Coach Casey. How could Coach think his amazing play-calling on the field and control of the game was "a failure"?

Brady was the most talented player on the team and the first-ever freshman captain in State's football history. He was the face of the program. He was the star.

Speaking of stars, he needed to text back his quickly expanding fan club. "Can't keep the A-listers waiting," he thought. But first, there were still a few autographs that he needed to sign.

CELL PHONE

There would be no adoring fans to greet him when he landed in the mountainous terrain. It would be just him and his cell phone. He was momentarily comforted by the fact that he could feel his phone in the left pocket of his jumpsuit. It was in a small baggie along with some other "just-in-case" essentials.

During his first deployment on an aircraft carrier, he'd forgotten to put his cell phone in a baggie. He learned that was a big mistake when you're on a boat - albeit a very large boat - in the middle of the ocean.

He was far from an ocean during this latest training period at the Naval Air Station, but it was still a good idea to play it safe. His cell phone was too important to mess around with. Today is had become his literal lifeline.

His first call once he found a signal was to HQ, but his second call was going to be to his mother. He was not scared, but this series of events make him think about her and maybe appreciate her a little bit more right now.

RECRUITING LETTER

Brady heard his mom's footsteps coming down the hall. "What did she want now?" he wondered.

"Honey, are you in there?"

"Yes, mom!"

Of course, Brady was in his room. Where else would he be after practice? She should know by now that every day he came home to hone his quarterbacking skills by playing some Madden Football on his gaming system. His dad used to rave about some archaic Atari game called Centipede, but for Brady's money, there would never be a better video game than Madden.

"Hey, dear, I just had to sign for a letter. I'll bring it to you."

"Thanks, mom, but just put it with all the others. I'm busy right now."

What started as a shoebox had turned into three large boxes full of recruiting letters, notes, and fancy brochures from nearly every school in the country. They all wanted the same thing ... to convince the top-rated sophomore recruit in the country to play quarterback for their football program one day.

He could still remember his first recruiting letter. He'd been the happiest eighth-grader in the world at that moment. Somebody wanted him, Brady Thomas, to be their quarterback one day.

As the months and football seasons ticked down, the euphoria of receiving letters was starting to wear off. The recruiting process and the constant sales pitches had become more of an annoyance than anything. Each recruiter said the same things. He knew he was going to be a starter wherever he went because he had a rare combination. He had elite talent and an unparalleled work ethic.

The stories of his work ethic were legendary. Since sixth grade, he'd worked with a passing coach every morning at 5:00 am to hone his skills. He could make all the throws - from delicate touch passes that could thread the needle between two defenders to missiles thrown a country mile - Brady made it look easy.

The passing coach brought in different ex-pros and local college guys to be the pass receivers during practice. The coach, an ex-pro player himself, wanted Brady to have every opportunity to maximize his potential as a quarterback.

The hours and money spent were a great investment as his talent was unquestioned and his potential was through the roof.

"I don't think you want me to put this letter in the box," his mother answered back to Brady through the closed door.

"Why, what's up?"

"It's from State, and I had to sign for it so it must be important."

Nearly every college in the nation wanted him. Every offer said the same thing: Full ride scholarship with the plan that he would be their starting quarterback his freshman year.

Every college, that was, except State.

Sure, some of Coach Casey's staff had reached out at different times and talked with him. They had come to some games, but they had never offered him a scholarship much less told him he'd start for them.

State had never sent anything special to Brady before. With his mother's announcement, he felt a twinge of that euphoria once again.

"State? Is it from the football team or just the school?"

"It's from the football program, Brady."

"Can you tell which coach?"

"Seriously, Brady! Pause the game, open the door, act like you're part of the human race, and come see for yourself. Mercy!"

The door opened, and Brady stood there wearing his sweats, cell phone in one hand, and the other extended out toward his mom.

Brady grabbed the envelope from his mom's hands in the nicest way possible - for a teenager.

"Thanks, mom!"

Quickly opening it, his face changed expressions from slight curiosity to a Kool-Aid smile filled with excitement.

"Well?" asked his mom. "You obviously like what the letter says. I assume it's an invite to their elite camp like you'd been hoping for?"

"Better than that, Mom. It's from Coach Casey. He's offering me a full ride. State wants me to play quarterback for them!"

"Congratulations, honey! I know this has been your dream. You've worked so hard, and you're going to be a superstar. It'll be awesome seeing those good college receivers catching your passes."

This was a great day for Brady, and he was glad his mother had always supported him.

"I'm so proud of you, honey. You put so much work in to achieve all of your goals. I'm glad to see that you're getting exactly what you had hoped to achieve."

LETTER FROM TOPGUN

The doorbell rang and Brady ignored it as usual. He knew his roommate would take care of whomever it was.

"Yo, Mav, a certified letter just came for you," Shorty shouted from the other room.

Brady's roommate was not actually named Shorty. At six feet, five inches, Rich Woodard was at the top end of height restrictions for a Naval aviator, hence, he received the call sign as a Junior Officer.

"Well, did you sign for it?" Brady asked.

"No, I said you're dead and to send it back where it came from."

"What?" replied Brady a little confused.

"Of course, I signed for it!" Rich said shaking his head.

"Who's it from?"

"Your mom," Shorty quickly snapped back.

"What?"

"Seriously dude, come get it. I'm not your butler, your maid, or your mailman."

Brady walked into the living room and took the letter from Shorty. He wasn't expecting it so soon, but he was excited to see the return address from the Naval Air Station in Fallon, Nevada.

TOPGUN!

Since watching Tom Cruise in one of his dad's favorite movies, *Top Gun*, he'd always wanted to be a fighter pilot. That was the goal after his playing days were over. Despite his physical talents, professional football didn't go as he'd anticipated.

He was on five different NFL rosters over three seasons, seeing action in only seven games. Eventually, the phone calls quit coming and so he turned his attention to his only other passion – flying jets.

He knew *Top Gun* was a Hollywood movie. Not everything portrayed was accurate, including the simple fact, the program was one word, not *Top Gun*. None of that kept Brady from wanting to sport the cool sunglasses, wear the TOPGUN patch, or fly daring missions at breakneck speeds.

His talent as a naval aviator had him moving up the ranks quickly. He was currently a lieutenant, but there was no doubt in Brady's mind that rank would be a thing of the past in no time.

Brady tore open the letter.

Lieutenant Thomas,
Thank you for applying to the Naval Fighter Weapons School at NAS Fallon. We regret to inform you that you have not been chosen as part of this year's incoming class.

There was more to the letter but there was no need to read anymore as he balled up the paper and whipped it against the wall.

Brady was fed up.

"TOPGUN is for the best of the best. That's me! I've been fast-tracked for promotions. My scores are off the charts. Who's more talented than me? How could I not get selected?"

"Dude, you'll be fine", said Shorty. "I'm sure most people don't get in on their first attempt."

Unfortunately, a similar scene would play out two more times despite Brady becoming a decorated war hero and achieving the rank of squadron captain.

To say Brady Thomas didn't understand the decision by TOPGUN would be an extreme understatement.

ALONE WITH HIS THOUGHTS

He had punched out only moments ago, but it seemed to take forever to finish the descent to solid ground. He would soon land in the middle of nowhere. His thoughts ran wild.

It wasn't that his life was passing before his eyes. He'd cleared the canopy and jet wash and now could see his trajectory would land him in a safe area. This fiasco pushed his thoughts towards his failure to be accepted at TOPGUN

His rejections were constantly on his mind, and the emotions were more extreme than usual.

He'd never been given an answer why a military hero and Navy Captain was rejected three times. The more he thought about it, the angrier and more frustrated he became.

If he was at TOPGUN right now, he wouldn't be in this predicament. Not because he wouldn't be flying training missions, but because there wouldn't be any plane malfunctions.

The guys at TOPGUN are the best of the best and that goes for the flight crew and maintenance personnel. "They wouldn't have screwed up like my guys did today!" Brady thought.

OFFENSIVE LINEMAN

The TV was showing a featured story about Lamar Jackson giving his offensive linemen Rolexes as a Christmas gift.

"Hey Brady, when are we getting our Rolexes?" asked Bo Lilja, State's left tackle.

"When boosters start paying me Lamar Jackson money or you guys start blocking like the Baltimore Ravens o-line. Whichever comes first."

"Maybe you should start asking for more money from your sugar daddies," Bo said with a laugh.

"It'd probably be easier if you guys got stronger, quicker, and smarter," Brady shot back.

He tried to make a joke of it, but there was too much truth in the fact that no college quarterback had been sacked more than Brady had that year. It's hard to throw touchdowns when you're lying on the ground.

"No big deal, brother. I still have the Rollie I bought in the Dominican for $25. Got a great deal. Bartered the kid down quite a bit. My business classes came in handy."

"I'm pretty sure it had nothing to do with your negotiating skills, big fella."

His guys were big but not all that good. Brady couldn't figure out why Coach Casey never recruited or developed better offensive linemen.

"If Coach isn't careful, I'll become another David Carr," Brady thought.

David Carr was the first-ever draft pick of the expansion Houston Texans. He was the first overall pick of the 2002 NFL Draft. He was everything you wanted from a quarterback. He was fast, had a strong arm, and a good head on his shoulders. But Houston had a terrible offensive line, and Carr got sacked 76 times during his rookie season. That was far and away the most in NFL history.

Brady didn't know whether it was Coach Casey's fault the line was bad or if the players themselves didn't care enough to improve. One thing was certain. Brady was not going to be giving these dudes any gifts until they earned them and started protecting him on the field.

PARACHUTE LANDING

He tried to land as smoothly as he could, but the rocky terrain of the mountain made it tricky. Fortunately, he safely made it to land and disconnected himself from the parachute.

Brady's top-of-the-line cell phone might have been one of his prized possessions, but it wasn't a NASA satellite phone.

His screen communicated a frustrating reality.

No bars. No service.

"Of course, there isn't any service," Brady thought. He was in the middle of nowhere with mountains on all sides.

Brady took a deep breath, exhaled, and shook his head. He couldn't believe his predicament. This stuff happens to other people.

He put his phone back in the baggie and then in his pocket. He surveyed the terrain and developed a game plan.

It probably wouldn't be long before the rescue team was assembled and en route to his location. They won't waste a lot of time when a Navy Cross recipient is missing. Brady was sure that his rescue would be a high priority.

His beacon would automatically alert them. However, as he looked around, he also realized the helicopter would have to be almost directly overhead to know exactly where he was.

They'd be coming soon, though not soon enough for his taste.

The sooner they get here, the sooner I can find out who screwed up.

He knew from experience that he had plenty of time to play the blame game while he played the waiting game.

He didn't want to wait, but football taught him how to be patient. How many hundreds of hours had he spent during his football career waiting in a locker room before a game?

TALKING WITH THE BACKUP

Brady had spent countless pre-games in a locker room preparing to go to battle, but for some reason, one such occurrence always stood out to him. It wasn't necessarily a good memory, but more of an irritating one that would surface every once in a while.

Though he had a million things he could and should be focused on right now, the thought of waiting brought that irritating memory into his head. Shaking his head, he couldn't believe this thought had just crept into his mind at a time like this.

"Hey Brady, I've got some questions about the new offensive package Coach put in for this game," said John Tyna. "Could you go over it with me?"

"Dude, you aren't going to need to know that stuff," Brady responded with a smirk. "Those plays are for me, not my backup. Come on man!"

"I know, but what if you get hurt? I've got to be prepared, right?"

"I haven't missed a game since seventh grade when my mom grounded me because I let my little brother get in trouble on the school bus."

"Seriously? That must have stunk."

"It did. I wanted to play so bad."

"No, I mean, it must have stunk to still be riding the bus in seventh grade." smiled John.

It wasn't often that freshman John Tyna got a chance to needle the senior.

"Yeah, funny guy. I thought it was funny that my little brother was screwing around on the bus. I could have stopped him, but I was laughing, and I wanted the little pest to get in trouble."

"Bad plan since you were the one that got punished."

"No kidding. My parents said I was my brother's keeper, and as the older brother, I needed to look after him."

Brady shook his head as the memories came back to him.

"Anyway, that concludes our trip down memory lane, but yes, that was the last time I had to sit out a game, so you have nothing to worry about. Even if we get up big and Coach puts you in during mop-up duty, you won't be running those plays. You'll just be handing the ball off to the running back on every snap trying to run out the clock."

"Thanks for the help, big brother," John said sarcastically.

"You're very welcome little brother. And by the way, I'm no stranger to sarcasm."

"That might be true, but you haven't quite grasped that 'brother's keeper' concept."

Brady added another layer of tape on his non-throwing wrist as he gave minimal thought to what John just said.

"Sure I have. I'm my brother's keeper right now. I'm keeping you safe, so your momma doesn't have to worry about you. Football can be a dangerous game, and I make sure I'm so good that you don't have to play and put yourself in harm's way," Brady said with a slight chuckle.

"You liked that one, didn't you? You're cracking yourself up," John said shaking his head. "That's sad."

"It is what it is, my brother. Just hop on and enjoy the ride. Let's have some fun this season. Who knows, maybe I'll bring you as my plus one to New York for the Heisman weekend."

"Ah, shucks. You'd do that for me, big brother."

"Yep, just follow me, and I'll lead you to the promised land."

"Seriously, do you ever listen to what comes out of your mouth?"
"Relax. You know I'm just messing with you."
"Sure you are."
"Yeah, besides, I'll probably take someone better looking than you to New York anyway."

John rolled his eyes.

STATUS REPORT

It was bad enough he had to punch out, but why couldn't it have been in wine country or out in the open? The terrain in the Sierra's was rocky and uneven.

He knew it would present a challenge to the rescue team. But for right now, he needed to find a safe and secure location to hole up.

Fortunately, he was not hurt. The ejection had been textbook, and his landing was just as he'd practiced in flight school.

He'd worked hard his whole life on the skills necessary for success. He felt he'd earned his success.

His flawless punch out today was a result of his composure in the cockpit and his attention to detail during training. The Navy requires its aviators to go through survival training every four years. This includes skills such as surviving in the water or escaping from a parachute.

He was not hurt, and he attributed that not to luck but his hard work and preparation.

Preparation had been the key to his successful playing career, too. Brady took care of his body and that had allowed him to avoid broken bones or torn ligaments. He could only remember one time during his career that he had succumbed to an injury. He wasn't even sure the concussion was something that he could have been prevented.

INJURY

Brady had just completed a pass to start the third quarter against their number one rival, but he got hit as he released the football.

"This does not look good as Brady Thomas is not getting up," the TV analyst said as the cameras were locked on the team captain laid out at midfield.

The replays showed the defensive end's hand coming down hard on the side of Brady's helmet as he was hitting him from his blindside.

Blows to the head were taken very seriously by medical personnel, and this was no exception.

As the trainers helped walk Brady to the sideline, it was apparent he had no idea where he was or even who he was at that moment. It wasn't known whether he'd been unconscious at any point, but he had been hit hard.

As Coach Casey returned to the sideline after attending to Brady, he called out for John Tyna.

John had already grabbed his helmet and started getting loose. Since Brady was being attended to by the medical staff, he was going to be out of the game for at least one play if not out for the whole second half.

"Okay, John" Coach said. "You're up. We don't need you to be Brady. You don't need to be the hero. Just do what you're capable of doing. Execute the game plan. The new package of plays worked great in the first half. We'll just pick up where we left off."

"Just execute the game plan," John thought. How ironic.

The offense broke the huddle and got set at the line of scrimmage. John took a deep breath and exhaled slowly. Anyone watching him closely would have thought he was trying to calm his nerves. He wasn't nervous in the traditional sense. He knew he had the talent to play at this level. His problem was his lack of preparation.

Just hours before, John and Brady had joked about this exact situation. Neither truly thought it would ever happen.

Despite what he thought, Brady never looked after his "little brother" to ensure the team's success, but John also hadn't studied the plays as hard as he should have. He'd gotten by on his talent all these years. Now he was unprepared to be thrust into action so quickly.

Several costly mistakes in the next few minutes caused the game to get out of hand. Before they knew it, State had let a slight halftime lead slip away, losing their one chance to make an early-season statement.

The freshman wasted little time dressing and leaving the stadium after his embarrassing performance and the difficult post-game press conference that followed.

RESCUE PLAN

Lieutenant Kopp looked around at his small team gathered in the briefing room.

"Any further questions?" he asked.

He didn't expect any questions as they had trained and prepared for these kinds of rescue missions, and they had successfully executed similar operations in the past.

Though every operation presented certain challenges, they always had a detailed game plan, which was owned by all the members. Each individual saw themselves as part of a team. To accomplish a mission and save lives, they all had to be on the same page. They even had a plan-B and contingencies for the contingencies. To say they were prepared would be an understatement.

Every Naval Air Station had this kind of team. The goal was for this team to be bored and underutilized. However, accidents occurred.

They were ready to go rescue Captain Thomas.

AT THE HOSPITAL

John arrived at the hospital and found Brady's room. The nurse allowed him to enter just as she finished jotting down his vital signs.

"How are you feeling, big brother," John asked with a smile.

"I'm lying in a hospital bed and my team just got whooped. How do you think I feel?" Brady responded, obviously frustrated.

Brady paused, looked up at the TV in the corner of the room, and then looked back at his backup.

"Big brother, huh?"

"Yeah, I was trying to be funny. Seriously though, how are you feeling? How's your head?"

"I'll live. I have a terrible headache, but at least I know where I am now. For a minute, I couldn't tell you what position I play much less what team I am on. That was pretty crazy!"

Brady continued, "I need to get cleared pretty quick. You guys need me. Fortunately, I put up some good numbers before I got jacked. Stinking Lilja. He let that dude get to me way too easily."

"It was rough today. Sorry, you ended up here. You were playing well. More than I could say for me."

"Don't sweat it. You just gotta be prepared next time. You can't be coming up to me at the last minute before a game asking those questions. You gotta take it more seriously. You always see me working on my game. I'm popular, but during the season you rarely see me out. There is time for that in the off-season. I'm committed to being the best. First to arrive, last to leave. Always watching more film. Always doing a little bit more. You have tons of talent, but you need to prepare if you want to win."

Brady grimaced and stopped talking as his head began to throb more. The Saturday night primetime game was on the TV, and they watched that for a few minutes in silence.

The freshman pondered what the senior star had just told him. Nothing he heard was surprising – or wrong. Much like Brady, he was the top recruit in the nation. He was brought in to learn the system from Brady for a year, but injuries to the two other backup quarterbacks on the roster led to John having to burn his redshirt year and be on the active roster.

The first half of the televised game ended, and the broadcast presented a special preview of the upcoming NFL season.

"Don't try to go out here and do everything for yourself," league MVP and Kansas City Chiefs quarterback Patrick Mahomes could be heard saying on the sidelines. "Believe in your teammates. Believe in each other."

Brady and John continued to listen as most of the analysts agreed the Chiefs were the team to beat yet again this season. Not only did the Chiefs have the talent, they noted, but they also made each other better. They were talented individuals that came together to be a great team, as opposed to just a collection of talent.

GREAT TEAMMATES

Great teams have great teammates. The commentator's statement resonated with John.

"You know, I've always gotten by on my talent," admitted John. "Lots of people compare you and me because we're similar in our abilities, but your work ethic makes us different."

"You'll get it," responded Brady. "You've got the rest of the season to watch how I work."

"Earlier when I called you my big brother, I was trying to be funny, but a part of me was also serious. I've always been the most talented person on the team. I've never had anyone that could push me or inspire me because nobody was on my level."

The backup looked up at the TV for a moment and then back at Brady.

"You told me that story about watching your little brother get into trouble on the bus. Well, you essentially let me get in trouble on the football field today. You didn't look out for me, man."

Brady started to say something, but John kept going.

"I know, I know, it's my fault I wasn't prepared. I choose to leave practice as soon as I can. It's my fault I have poor work habits. But man, would it have killed you to work with me a little bit this week or check in on me, or even take it halfway serious today in the locker room when I was cramming to understand the playbook?"

John continued, "You get most of the practice reps, and I'm struggling to get the regular playbook down, let alone the new stuff specific to today's game. I've never felt more uncomfortable in my life on a football field than I did today."

"Man, it's not that complicated," Brady responded. "You're a good enough player. You could have figured it out."

"That's not the point. Yes, I should have put in more time. I admit that," John said trying hard not to get too frustrated, especially since with Brady's concussion, the words probably sound twice as loud as normal. "The fact is, I need your help. Today was a wake-up call."

"As I said, watch what I do. Follow my lead. That's all you have to do."

"I've noticed you do that a lot. Do you think Mahomes would do that?"

"What do you mean? I hear he works hard."

"Yeah, me too, but I also hear that he works WITH his receivers constantly, so they all get better at the same time. He works WITH his linemen and backs so they're all on the same page."

John paused almost as if he was unsure how to say this next part.

"I honestly have never been around a harder worker than you, but the time you put in only benefits you. Weights, extra throwing, film sessions, all that stuff you do by yourself or with a trainer. You don't help your teammates get better. We might see your example, but some of us might not know how to translate what we see into reality. I know it sounds weird, but we aren't all wired like you."

The freshman was still a bit apprehensive sharing his thoughts with Brady, but he also wasn't sure he'd ever get another chance. Plus, he was not in the best of moods, either.

"I know you lift and train hard, but it's not with the rest of the team. It's at different times. You have your own personal film sessions with the coaches while they're at the office. But maybe you should bring in some receivers or linemen or me so we can watch together, learn together.

"I love what the commentators said about the best quarterbacks in the NFL," John said pointing to the TV. "It's not just about being the best but making their teammates and the team the best. Great teams have great teammates."

Brady was not happy being lectured by a freshman, especially one that wasn't a hard worker. On top of all that, he had to listen to this with a ringing in his head. Talk about bad timing.

"Are you saying I'm not a good teammate?" asked Brady.

"Listen, I'm far from perfect," said John. "I already admitted that my work ethic is suspect. I don't have a great understanding of what it takes to succeed at the college level. This is the first time in my entire life that I've sat on the bench. It's a different view being behind someone on the depth chart. Just like you, I've been the star, the leader, the captain my whole life, even in basketball and baseball. I've been blessed with athletic ability just like you."

John paused for a moment to try and collect his thoughts. He knew that he was overstepping the boundary, especially for a freshman. He knew he should show more respect to the senior, considering Brady was in the hospital for a concussion. But John had just failed his team in what was arguably the worst performance of his life. If he wanted to be a better leader of this team, he needed to analyze and understand what exactly went wrong today. A lot of the blame could be placed on him, but not all of it.

"I've picked up on something these last few weeks. I'm not ready for prime time yet. I have a long way to go. But I've also learned that we need to be a team. We can't win by ourselves. Our conference is too good. The competition is too good. You're the star. You're awesome man! But you can't do it all by yourself. Look at what happened today."

John was a freight train now and could not be stopped. He was going to get all of this off his chest. Fortunately for Brady, there was light at the end of the tunnel, and John only had one more thought to share.

"Regardless of the reason or whose fault it is, I wasn't ready today. We lost. Our team lost. Yes, you weren't there, and I am sorry for that. Just like you, I've always wanted to play for State and lead them to victory, but not like this. I don't want to play just because you're hurt. But you did get hurt, and we all should have been able to step up. It's obvious that you're the center of this team and without you on the field, we didn't get the job done. It was more my fault than anyone else's, but what if you're still out for the next game? Or even if you're able to play, but not yet 100 percent and have a bad game? Will the rest of the team know how to step up? How can we, as quarterbacks and leaders of the team, help everyone be better?"

Brady had reached his breaking point. He was glad John was finally passionate about something. Maybe this would be the start of a stronger work ethic. Maybe these last few minutes of his emotional tirade would inspire him. But right now, Brady needed some sleep. If not sleep, then at least peace and quiet.

"I hear you, little brother. I will take it all under consideration, but now I need to get some sleep. You're welcome to stay here and finish watching the game, but I've got to rest my brain or whatever is left of it after that hit today."

FLIGHT SUIT

It was amazing how dark it could get at night without the glow of street and security lights. Fortunately, Brady was prepared for situations like this. His desire to be the best at everything motivated him to train hard and be ready. He'd rarely experienced failure.

Star quarterback. Fighter pilot. Naval Captain. It didn't matter. He expected success. More importantly, he felt he deserved the success. He'd paid his dues.

The NFL hadn't worked out for Brady, but it all seemed worth it when the Admiral had pinned that medal to his uniform.

"Football Star Awarded Navy Cross" the headlines read.

It might not have been the NFL, but he was still the star. It might not be on the gridiron, but people still knew his name. Brady Thomas was a war hero.

Not only was he talented, famous, and brave, but he was alive.

A quarter of present-day Navy Cross recipients died in combat. Many Navy Cross recipients request privacy and don't want any kind of announcements made public. Because of that, the Navy Cross might represent heroism, but it can also symbolize the ultimate sacrifice.

Brady felt lucky to be alive after his heroic mission, but he'd never been ashamed of being awarded the Navy Cross even though it was the result of others not returning home.

He felt that he'd earned everything he'd ever accomplished.

THE CAPTAIN

He was talented and always prepared.

It might seem like a small thing, but his preparations would pay off now as he waited for the rescue team.

The Navy provided their aviators with regular training and the latest survival gear.

Brady was glad to have such a top-notch flight suit. It reminded him of all the top-of-the-line stuff State used to have access to.

TEAM TRAVEL SUIT

The players were excited for the first day together at fall camp. As the players walked into the meeting room after lunch, Coach Casey grabbed Brady.

"Hey Brady, we just received new gear. It's been a nightmare getting this order, but we got the first shipment just this morning, so we'll take it."

"That's great, Coach."

"Yes, except they sent the wrong sizes."

"That stinks. Sorry."

"I know. That's what I wanted to talk to you about. I need your help."

"Okay. You want me to grab some guys and carry it in?"

"No, it's already in the room."

Coach took a moment to wave to a couple of other players as they opened the doors to the meeting room and then turned his attention back to his senior captain.

"We are only missing a couple of travel suits, but I wanted to make sure that a couple of the freshmen got them in the right sizes so they start camp on the right foot. I think it would put you in an even better light as a captain if you were volunteer to go without for a day or two."

Brady looked confused and started to say something, but Coach Casey continued.

"I know this is a weird request, but you have top-of-the-line gear already and these freshmen, in particular John, don't have anything yet. Our dealer has assured me that he will fix the mistake, and we'll have the rest of the travel suits here within two to three days. We don't have any official functions this week, so we don't have to worry about looking all the same. When the final shipment comes in, you'll get this year's version. It's only for a couple of days. You okay with that?"

Coach Casey was normally spot on in evaluating body language, and he was getting the vibe that Brady was not convinced, nor concerned, that this issue was his problem.

"Hmmm, not really Coach. I guess I understand that you want them to have the right sizes and to keep John happy since he'll be taking over when I'm gone, but why does it have to be me? I want to be rocking the new swag. I'd think of all the guys on the team, I'd be the one the apparel company would want to wear their clothes. You want me representing State, right?"

"I'm sure the apparel company will be thrilled when you're seen wearing their travel suit. But despite being the preseason Heisman Trophy favorite, the paparazzi are not following you or your teammates that closely during fall camp. Our workouts are off-limits to media, and I know you don't go clubbing. You can go a few days wearing last year's uniform or any of the designer clothes you have custom made."

"I hear you, Coach, but I still don't understand why it has to me. There are plenty of other guys that are John's size."

"Brady, apparently I am not being very clear with you. It's not about being the same size. Yes, I could ask your teammates, but I'm asking you. It's not because I dislike you. It's not because I don't want you 'representing', as you say. I think you could greatly benefit yourself and the team by setting an example early on. I think you could show some real leadership with this small sacrifice by taking one for the team."

Brady was confused and more than a little frustrated with Coach Casey, who was well-respected nationally and knew the game inside and out. Even though he'd made Brady the program's first-ever freshman offensive captain, it seemed that Brady could never do anything right. It seemed like Coach Casey expected perfection. Brady was the most talented player, as well as the hardest worker on the team. What more did he want?

"Coach. What are you talking about? You made me the captain. People know that I'm the leader."

"Yes, Brady, you're the team captain. You're the star. You're the face of our program. But none of that automatically equals real leadership."

It wasn't lost on Brady that Coach Casey seemed to place extra emphasis on the word *REAL*. He didn't know what Coach was getting at, but it was irritating, nonetheless.

"With all due respect, Coach, I think I am a real leader. I'm the hardest worker on the team. I lay it on the line every day. I bust my tail at every workout. I grind the film. The guys see that."

"I am not questioning your work ethic, Brady, but sometimes being a leader is more than just making yourself better. Being a leader includes making others better."

"Okay, but how does giving my travel suit to a freshman make him better? Shouldn't he have to earn it? Doesn't having to wait to teach him patience or endurance or resiliency or any one of those 'cool' words you throw around all the time?" Brady said with a Cheshire cat grin.

"The message you send to the team when you make a personal sacrifice is different than the message sent by working hard. Both are equally important. If you, Captain Brady Thomas, are willing to do something like this, it tells your teammates that this should not be below them either. Before you know it, everyone is thinking of and helping each other, and our team culture becomes truly about the team and not the success of each individual."

"I get that, Coach," Brady started to say.

Once again, Coach Casey interrupted Brady, "Based on your body language and or insistence that I should not be asking this of you, I am pretty sure you do NOT get it. You're looking for excuses and rationale to resist this idea. Listen, you don't have to give up your travel suit. Wear it with pride these next few days. I will find someone else who is willing to sacrifice for our team. I thought this was the perfect opportunity for you to set the tone and send a message that you're a team player and expect the same from everyone else."

"I don't know coach... I'd think that I'd be the one the apparel company would want to wear their stuff. Isn't there any other guy that can give up his gear? Plus, I feel like I've paid my dues. Shouldn't a freshman have to earn something around here?"

"Say no more, Brady. Forget I asked. Go ahead and get into the meeting."

"Sorry, Coach. I hope you're not mad."

"I'm not mad, Brady. I'm just disappointed but thank you for clarifying your thought process."

Coach Casey thought, "He possesses so many important individual leadership qualities, but after all these years, he still doesn't understand what real leadership looked like. Such a waste of potential!" Would he ever get through to this kid?

JACKIE ROBINSON

Brady turned to walk away from Coach Casey and saw his roommate leaning against a wall. He'd been waiting a few feet away the entire time.

"Fun conversation there, Captain?" he asked Brady sarcastically.

"You heard that mess?" Brady asked rhetorically. "Whatever man. Let's go get a drink. We still have a few minutes before the meeting begins."

"You don't have to ask me twice. They sure stocked up the cooler with all kinds of drinks this year, didn't they?"

The two of them went over to the drink room. It reminded them of a convenience store since it had glass-encased coolers from wall to wall.

Lance Prater was one of the few guys on the team that Brady respected. They played on rival teams in high school but got to know each other well as they attended summer elite camps together. As a football player, Lance was as tough as they came. He was fearless. As a tight end, he had great hands and could run like the wind. Everyone seemed to like him, and he was a natural-born leader. He would probably be a CEO, big-time lawyer, or a politician one day after his NFL days were complete.

"Remember when we watched '42' last year on that road trip?" Lance asked while sipping on his sports drink.

"Yeah, good movie. Chadwick Boseman was awesome in his role as Jackie Robinson."

"You're right. He was a great actor and did a good job of portraying Jackie. I know there were a lot of layers to the movie but there was a leadership lesson that stood out to me when it came to Jackie's teammate, Pee Wee Reese."

"Okay, yeah. He was Jackie's friend. I get it. I should be kind and caring and compassionate and sensitive and understanding and all those other nice things," said Brady with a smile.

"Come on man. I'm not talking about that. It's not necessarily about friendships, though that can't hurt. It's about using our platform for good. Using our status for good. It's about using our power for good. To a degree, we all like having status and power and I know for sure that you like being everybody's All-American. But think of the good that you – or me for that matter – could do with it? We can use our platform for good."

Lance hesitated for a moment and when Brady didn't immediately respond, he continued. "Remember in the movie how Jackie made that error at second base and the crowd started booing and calling him all sorts of names? Remember, that was his own crowd. Crazy!"

"Yeah, that sucked. I expect to get rough treatment when we are in someone else's stadium, but I wouldn't know what to do if our fans started booing me," said Brady.

"I'm sure you could handle it. You'd probably feed off of it and it'd get you fired up. But not everyone is like you. This happened to Jackie. He was new. He didn't have status yet. Think if this happened on our team to a freshman or any other teammate that wasn't as confident as you?"

Lance continued, "Remember when Pee Wee Reese went over to Jackie and put his arm around him. The crowd stopped booing because Pee Wee Reese was their beloved favorite player. They couldn't boo him. That guy used his popularity for good."

Brady shook his head up and down, "I had kind of forgotten about that scene. It was cool."

"Not just cool but real. That kind of stuff can happen. It did happen. Coach told me the scene was true and not just some Hollywood creation. But anyway, not everyone has that kind of pull – that kind of power – but Pee Wee did."

They sat there for what seemed like forever but after three seconds, it was up to Lance, once again to break the silence and lead the conversation.

"You have that kind of power, Brady. You can make things happen. Unfortunately, you made things happen, but just for you. You used your power to benefit you instead of helping."

"What do you mean Lance? What did I do? How did I make things happen for me?"

Lance smiled shaking his head back and forth.

"Man, just go give Johnny boy your travel suit. It's not a big deal but it's a small Pee Wee Reese moment for you to use your power in just a small way."

"Whatever man. Didn't know you were all of a sudden, our locker room lawyer. Sure, I'll do it if it'll make you happy."

"Yes, it'll make me happy," said Lance. "But it's also the right thing to do."

"I don't know about it being the right thing," said Brady shaking his head and smiling. "But if it'll get you to stop nagging me. I'll go get it for him."

WEATHER GETS BAD

His fighter jet destroyed.
No cell phone reception.
Alone in God knows where.
Can this day get any worse?

No sooner had this thought crossed Brady's mind, he felt the first drop of rain. The second drop of rain soon followed and before it even sank in with Brady, the heavens seemed to open up and he was now wet as it poured down on him.

He quickly focused on what he needed to do and acted with a sense of urgency. For a moment, he'd forgotten about the blame game he was playing and went into survival mode. Since this was not during wartime, his survival was not the life-or-death type. It was more of a practical mindset of setting up his shelter and trying to keep from getting completely drenched.

His training and knowledge seemed to kick in automatically as he quickly found a small cave – an overhang, really – that would temporarily protect him from the downpour. The weather was, suddenly, his newfound opponent.

The seats of an FA-18 are like a Swiss army knife in a way. It's not all padding. The seats are loaded with survival supplies, so Brady had pretty much everything he needed. The U.S. Navy was good at preparing and having contingency plans for various situations.

The rain was an inconvenience, especially on this chilly December day.

Brady set up his makeshift shelter and unfolded the blanket. He didn't need this rain right now. He wondered if it would turn to sleet or snow. Even if it did, it probably wouldn't be until later tonight and he'd be rescued by then.

He figured he only had to put up with this annoyance of rain for another hour or so at the most. But unknown to Brady, the weather would soon take a turn for the worse.

SNOWY FOOTBALL GAME

Brady had played in the cold before, but he couldn't remember playing in this bad of weather. Mother Nature continued to wreak havoc on this dreary day in early December. The snow flurries had started that morning and had only intensified as the day went along.

"This is it," the television announcer said. "This is the last chance for State to avoid the upset. It has not been the season they've been expecting but nobody thought it would end like this."

"Alright, guys. We've looked stupid so far, but we can still redeem ourselves," said Brady as he entered the huddle.

His offensive teammates looked back at him shivering and with looks of discouragement in their eyes. Sure, they would like to march the length of the field in these last 90 seconds, but for many of them, they'd probably rather be back in the locker room taking a warm shower.

Brady picked up on this vibe. But truth be told, he wasn't mad at the guys. As soon as the final gun sounded, he'd do some of the quickest post-game handshakes in history and probably beat many of his teammates into the locker room and get out of these cold, wet clothes.

As the television cameras zoomed in on the huddle, millions of fans across the country were none the wiser at Brady's thoughts as they listened to the announcers.

"This is the kind of situation that a competitor like Brady Thomas lives for. Statistically speaking, he has had a historic season and will most likely win the Heisman, but the team has struggled. If he can take his teammates down the field, State would finish with a .500 record and avoid the first losing season in three decades."

A graphic flashed across the screen letting the viewers know that only two times in the history of the Heisman has a player won the award without playing on a winning team – Jay Berwanger, the first-ever winner in 1935, and Hall of Famer Paul Hornung in 1956.

Despite the team's mediocre record, the commentators seemed to believe in Brady.

"Joe Montana, Drew Brees, and Russell Wilson, these are all guys that have orchestrated legendary comebacks. You've got to think Brady Thomas is down there firing up his guys for one last effort to save this season."

Brady relayed the play to his teammates. They would be conducting their two-minute drill for the rest of the game. Each player would already know their assignments in this organized form of chaos.

Essentially it would be like the millions of friends and relatives across the country playing backyard football on a Thanksgiving afternoon. Just get open.

"Just get open and I'll hit you," Brady said with little enthusiasm and even less confidence.

Just get open, Brady thought ... so you can drop another pass.

The day had been miserable from a weather standpoint but also a performance standpoint. Brady hadn't even completed half of his passes that day. He had also thrown more interceptions than touchdowns in those snowy conditions.

THE CAPTAIN

As the team broke the huddle, he watched the receivers run to their spots and wondered how it was that he was surrounded by so many guys that weren't any good.

Clocks have better hands than these wide receivers he thought to himself. A slight smirk appeared on his face just for a moment as he came to the line of scrimmage and prepared to take the snap from the center.

Two completions and three dropped passes later, State was not much closer to scoring. They were still 65 yards away from the end zone with just seven seconds left on the clock.

They would need a miracle. It was time for a Hail Mary throw.

As Brady took the snap, he ran to his right to buy himself some extra time. There was no question that he had the arm strength to throw it three-quarters of a football field accurately. The only question would be whether his receivers could make a play and catch the ball in the end zone.

He'd done this plenty of times during his career. But as he planted his foot, he forgot about the havoc that mother nature had been wreaking on the field all day.

As he planted his foot, the cleats he was wearing didn't stick in the ground like normal. The snow made the ground very slippery, and his foot kept going to the right toward the sidelines, which meant his body also went in that direction.

Instead of giving his receivers one last chance to salvage the day, he fell to the ground awkwardly as he fumbled the ball for the second time that afternoon.

The game was over and so was the season.

Brady couldn't believe his bad luck. The weather had played havoc on his day. The conditions didn't allow his talents to shine.

The thought never entered his mind the other quarterback played in the same conditions that day.

DELAYED RESCUE

The Navy was equipped with the most advanced technology and this satellite imaging was not providing good news for the individuals at the Naval Air Station trying to organize a rescue.

"Sir, the weather front we had mentioned to you earlier is worse than we thought," said the ranking member of the rescue team.

"What does that mean for getting your team airborne and getting Captain Thomas?"

"Quite simply, we can't do it. It's not a hurricane or anything like you went through a few years ago when you were at Norfolk but it's bad."

Lieutenant Kopp paused for a moment. He was never one to accept defeat and even now was trying to come up with a solution to this problem.

"If we were in a combat situation, I'm not sure we could justify sending our team out there. It's just too risky. But since he's not in danger of capture and we know he has the survival gear to handle this storm, we're going to need to wait until the weather lets up a little bit."

"Thanks for letting me know. I'd like a situation report every 30 minutes for the rest of the evening. Though it's not a combat situation, we still don't want one of our guys out there any longer than he needs to be – especially a guy like Captain Thomas. The longer it goes, the more likely the media gets word and then we have a new set of issues. War hero. Heisman Winner. He's not just a typical pilot."

"Yes, sir. Understood. I'll let you know immediately if things change, and we might be able to lift off but, in the meantime, I'll provide those sit reps to you personally every 30 minutes."

As Lieutenant Kopp left the room, he hoped the next report he delivered would be while on the way to the chopper with the mission green-lighted for go.

HEISMAN WINNER

The master of ceremonies paused as he opened the envelope that would reveal this year's winner.

"And this year's recipient of the season's Most Outstanding Player award goes to..."

Cheers erupted throughout the banquet room as Brady's name was announced and he walked up to the podium to accept the award.

"Wow! I'd like to thank the committee, the Athletic Club, all the voters, the corporate partners, my teammates, and coaches. This is quite an honor."

Brady continued, "Ever since I was a little kid, I wanted to be the best quarterback in the nation. It's amazing to think how I was able to do that and also to play for State. What a dream come true."

After a few more minutes, Brady wrapped up his speech and was led backstage to talk with reporters. Some of his friends and family members had also gathered in a side room adjacent to the banquet hall.

The first few questions were fairly standard for an award winner. But then Brady started to get some questions that he was not quite ready for, and quite frankly, didn't understand why they were being asked.

"You mentioned that you always wanted to play for State but are you concerned with how you left the program?"

THE CAPTAIN

"I'd say I left it pretty good. I won this award, didn't I?" Brady responded.

"Yes, you did but this was the first time that State has ever had a four-year period without a bowl win," the reporter followed up. "Your stats improved every year, but the team's win total did not. How do you explain that?"

Brady was trying to stay composed on this exciting and memorable day, but he was starting to get perturbed with this reporter.

"That was unfortunate, but football is still a team sport. I did what I was able to do but I'm not the only guy out there. It takes more than one person to lose a game. Every guy needs to do their part. I did my part. It's unfortunate that we couldn't have won more."

Another reporter had a question.

"Piggybacking on the last question ... would you agree that State underachieved the last few years? State had won conference titles in four of the five years before your arrival but now has gone four straight years without a title. Despite all of your records and accomplishments, do you have an opinion on why you guys weren't able to capitalize on that recent success?"

"It's a battle every Saturday. I played hard. I competed hard. I did my job. I don't know what else you guys are looking for. I feel like you're blaming me for our losses. The results weren't what I was hoping for, but I tried to do my part every time I took the field. I wish we'd won more. I do. I don't know what to tell you."

Brady didn't let a few overzealous reporters get to him. This was the day that he'd dreamed of all his life. He was the best player in college football. The last few questions were much more friendly and typical of an awards ceremony.

RESCUE TEAM IS A GO

It wasn't quite time for an update, so the base commander was hopeful that Lieutenant Kopp had good news when he entered the room.

The base commander's optimism was rewarded.

"Sir, it looks like we've got a window of opportunity for the next few hours to rescue Captain Thomas."

The base commander was relieved. Not only did he have a great group of pilots, but his support personnel were top-notch. The rescue team was no exception.

"Great. Let's go get him. Good luck lieutenant."

As they had been analyzing the situation constantly, they believed Brady was not in immediate danger, so they weren't going to gamble with the lives of the rescue team. But now that the weather had broken for the better, they sprang into action and wasted little time getting their helicopter off the ground.

BRADY'S RESCUE

Though someone as talented as Captain Thomas would never lose track of time in a situation like this, Brady had allowed his mind to wander a bit, which made time seem to pass quicker than normal.

He was playing the blame game to perfection right now. As great of a football player he was, his skills at playing the victim and pointing mental fingers at others were elite. It was never his fault. He just couldn't comprehend that anyone else could be as talented or work as hard as him.

Despite playing the blame game, Brady made sure to do what he could to facilitate his rescue. Despite the rocky terrain, Brady had found an area that seemed flat enough for the rescue helicopter.

As the helicopter landed, Brady was both relieved to be one step closer to having this ordeal over and perturbed as to why he had to wait so long for help to arrive.

Despite not being hurt, Brady still let the rescue team come to him.

He did allow himself a smile as he saw the way the rescue team members sprinted from the helicopter and to his current location. It was like they were being timed in the 40-yard dash at the NFL combine.

"Captain Thomas, I'm Lieutenant Kopp. Are you okay?"

"Yes, I'm fine. Let's just get out of here. Took you guys long enough."

"Sorry, sir. The bird was grounded this whole time. We were ready but we just couldn't get up in the air. Your weather here wasn't good, but it was even worse on the other side of the mountain. Zero visibility. We couldn't risk it. There was no way we could endanger the crew, sir. But we're very glad that you're okay."

Brady wasn't very satisfied with that answer. He was someone that just got things done and found a way. If that rescue team or that chopper pilot were that good, they could have made it work. Brady struggled with understanding any perceived incompetence in others.

"Sir, we're going to take you to a nearby hospital before returning to base. It's only a few minutes away and we need to make sure that there are no internal injuries you might have suffered."

"I said I'm fine."

"Yes sir. We understand. We just want to make sure. Plus, you're lucky the hospital closest to our location happens to be one of the best."

"I'm just frustrated lieutenant. I've been waiting a long time for you and now that you're here, I still can't go back to base."

"Yes sir. We understand. We'll have you to the hospital soon and hopefully, you'll get good news once they check you out. We'll try to make the ride as smooth and fast as we can."

"Yes sir, but we're a team. I might make the calls, as you say, but those calls affect more than just me. We have awesome and talented individuals on this crew, but we're all responsible for one another. We have each other's backs and understand that every mission requires all of us, no matter how talented any one of us might be. We win together. We overcome challenges together."

Brady started to tune out the young lieutenant as he started sounding a lot like someone else, he knew.

EX-BACKUP IN THE NFL

John Tyna took questions from the reporters gathered in front of his locker.

"It was a total team effort out there today," said Tyna. "I'm so proud of our guys."

Shorty looked up from his grill duties to peek at the television.

"Hey Mav, wasn't that dude your backup at State," asked Shorty. "Why's he in the NFL and you're hanging out with us on this fine Sunday afternoon?"

"Well, I'm not here because of your barbecuing skills that's for sure," Brady teased as he continued cutting his steak that was fresh off the grill.

The guys had been watching another game but were now channel surfing and stopped when they saw John Tyna being interviewed. They knew that it was a thorn in Brady's side that Tyna was in the NFL, and he wasn't.

It wasn't very often they could needle everybody's all-American, the hero, the captain, Brady Thomas.

They weren't in a hurry to find another game as long as Brady's former backup was on the TV talking. The seven-time Pro Bowl quarterback had suffered an injury a few weeks ago but continued to take questions from reporters.

"It looks like you'll be ready to come back soon, maybe even next week. Have you been given clearance by the medical staff to return to action next week?" Tyna was asked.

"Yes, I have been cleared to suit up and will be available if needed."

"If needed. What does that mean? Are you or are you not able to play?

"Yes, I can play. The training staff has done a great job of getting me ready and the rehab has gone great. I couldn't ask for a better group of people to work with. They've got me all healed up. Better than new," he said with a big smile.

The reporter still wanted clarification on the situation. "So, you'll take your place back in the starting lineup, right?"

"That's not my decision. It's not my job. My job is to get prepared and to help my teammates get ready for next Sunday. We're trying to make the playoffs again and I'm going to do everything I can to help us achieve that goal."

"But John, it sounds like you're saying you might not start on Sunday even though you're healthy. The unwritten rules say that starters don't lose their spot because of injury. Have you discussed this with the coaching staff yet?"

"Yes, we've talked throughout this process. But we also had discussions before the injury. Our conversations are always centered around what's best for the team, what's the best game plan, and how we can best prepare for our next opponent. That hasn't changed whether I'm hurt or not. Even when I've been hurt these last few weeks, I've continued to go to every position meeting and watch film with the guys. I've prepared like I was going to play even though I wasn't even going to be in uniform. It's my responsibility to provide a good example and it's also my responsibility to help the team."

"I think we all understand that and can appreciate that," a reporter followed up. "But all we're trying to find out is whether you plan on taking first-team reps this week and starting on Sunday?"

"I appreciate the question and the job you have to do as reporters. Dak has done an amazing job and we're 3-0 with him starting. He's performing exactly the way we hoped when the organization drafted him. Just like it was my responsibility to help the team win ever since I was drafted. We have a culture that looks at things that way, which is why we're consistently in the playoffs."

John paused for a moment as he thought about how fortunate he was to play for a team that did things the right way.

"Sure, I want to play. I always do what I can to prepare myself and make myself better. But ultimately my responsibility isn't just to be a starter, but rather to do whatever I can to help our team win. Every team in the league has a starting quarterback but not every team makes the playoffs. It's not about starting. It's about the team."

John continued, "Before I got hurt, I'd help Dak prepare just in case he went into the game. I'd help the offensive linemen understand the game plan better. I'd stay after practice and throw balls to the receivers if they wanted extra work. I'm not saying any of this to brag. I'm saying it because that is what the quarterback should do. That is what any leader should do. As a leader, it's not about me. I have a responsibility to help my team be the best it can be."

Brady was getting irritated listening to the interview with his former backup.

"Can someone turn the channel so we can watch some real football?" Brady asked shaking his head. "Blah, blah, blah. Seriously! This is like some major Tony Robbins feel-good motivational type stuff at this press conference."

"In a minute, Mav. Besides, I'd think you'd like this stuff since you're a leader," said a smiling Shorty as he put the word 'leader' in air quotes and then saluted his long-time friend.

TAKING RESPONSIBILITY

Shorty never seemed to disappoint on the grill. The steak was cooked just right. Brady had an easy time cutting it and savored the tender meat.

However, Brady didn't quite enjoy what he was watching on the big screen. For Brady, the wound cut deep as his former backup had made it big. He seemed like the perfect quarterback now. John had come a long way from his days at State.

"Sure, I want to be out there next week. All competitors want to play. But it's not about me and what I want. It's about what's best for the team. I know that sounds all cliché but it's true. I certainly didn't always think that way. When I was in high school or even early on in my college career, I might have thought it was all about me. I might have thought that if I was a better player, then the team would be better. However, that's not the case. When you're part of a team, what one guy does affects everyone else. What they do can affect me, as well. I gradually learned that we need to have each other's backs and make each other better if we want to have any chance at achieving our team goals."

Reporters love controversy and they'd rather have John stirring something up with his backup Dak, but there was something so genuine about what John was saying. Even though this was the first time they'd heard him say it, judging from his past actions, nobody doubted his sincerity.

"Something magical is happening to this team right now," John continued. "Not only have we won three in a row with Dak but it's the way we've won. There is excitement, and everyone can feel it. This can be a special season. As I said, it wasn't my fault I got hurt but if I become a distraction to this team or fail to help my teammates because of my agendas, then that is my fault. I'm going to have Dak's back and if I'm the one out there playing, then I know he's going to have my back, as well. That's what leaders do. That's what great teammates do."

"From the time that I was young, it was emphasized that the quarterback wins and loses games. That is not necessarily true. There are lots of reasons a team wins and losses. But I do believe one hundred percent that I'm responsible for helping my team win or lose whether I'm on the field or not. Today we won and I didn't play a snap, but I was responsible for helping us win. Four weeks ago, when I played in my last full game and we won, Dak was responsible for helping us win even though he didn't play an entire snap."

The team's beat reporter tried to get to the bottom line to help out his readers.

"We get all that and we're glad that we get to cover you," said the reporter. "It's refreshing to have a star player have that kind of attitude, but can you tell us what your plans are for this week? What will be your process? How will the starter be decided?"

"I'm not Coach, but I imagine the process and the decision-making will be similar to how it is every week. All 53 of us guys get what we earn within the framework of what's best for the team. Football is a meritocracy. Nothing is handed to any of us ... at least on good teams, that is. You earn everything, every single day, over and over again. You have to prove it. What's best for the team? As of right now, Dak has earned the right to keep leading this team on the field. He's earned

Taking Responsibility

the right to be our quarterback. As a competitor, it's hard for me to say that, but he's earned that right."

John continued, "I will continue to push him and challenge him on the field, in film sessions, and meetings. Not so I can take his job but so that I can help make both of us better. When we're both better, our team is better. I can't control what decisions Coach makes but I can control my actions and whether I'm being a good leader or just looking out for my desires. Agendas turn talented teams into afterthoughts. Agendas can turn us into an under-achieving bunch of individuals. We don't want that for this team. We're different."

Knowing the schedule of the guys for the rest of the day, the team's media director stepped in.

"Thanks for everyone's questions today. John has got to run. He has a few other team obligations as you can imagine."

And with that, the reporters were ushered away from his locker so that he could finish getting dressed and get to his next rehab session.

Shorty didn't know when he'd get another chance to needle his friend like this, so he took his shot.

"Hey Mav, didn't that dude take over for you during your senior year when you got hurt?" asked Shorty.

"Yeah, but it was only for a game and a half."

"That was one heck of a speech he just gave to those reporters. Did he learn all that from you?" joked Shorty. "You must have been his role model."

Brady finished chewing his bite of steak.

"Nope ... I never gave a speech quite like that."

HELICOPTER TAKES OFF

It was obvious the helicopter pilot enjoyed his job enough to joke at a time like this. Just like it was hard to be mad at Shorty for all of his joking, it seemed to be equally difficult for Brady to be mad at that pilot with the big toothy grin.

"Welcome to our home away from home, Captain Thomas," shouted the helicopter pilot as the rescue team helped Brady into the chopper.

"We're glad you're okay. We'll have you to the hospital in no time. Now just sit back, relax, make sure your tray tables are up, and your cell phone is on helicopter mode."

Brady would try to relax for the next few minutes as this nightmare seemed to be coming to a close. He'd survived the mountains and now just needed to survive his next battle – the hospital.

The large mountains got smaller and smaller as the helicopter ascended into the clouds and Brady peered out of the window.

SEQUOIA HOSPITAL

The attending nurse greeted Brady as he entered the hospital.

"Captain Thomas, welcome to Sequoia Hospital," she said. "We'll take good care of you as we get you checked out."

Like most athletes, Brady hated hospitals. To many Alpha types like Brady, they represented illness, sickness, and weakness. If he was at a hospital then he was sick, ill, or weak and he didn't want to be any of those.

"Thanks, but like I told the team that picked me up, I'm good."

"Yes, sir, but we've been informed that this is necessary for all pilot accidents," the nurse said.

"Alright, let's get this over with. What do you need from me?"

"Well, sir, we'll be running a few tests. Please try to relax and answer all of our questions honestly. We'll try to get you out of here as soon as we can. You'll just need to be patient for a few minutes until we can get some x-rays and cat scans."

"Sounds like loads of fun."

"It'll be fine, sir. We have a great team here at Sequoia that will take care of you."

THE DOCTOR

Even though Brady didn't appear to be hurt, the hospital wasted little time sending a doctor to check in on him.

"Captain Thomas, I'm Dr. Decipeda. We're going to do a few routine tests and look you over just to make sure that everything is okay."

"No problems here, Doc. Not injured but I do have a severe case of frustration. I'm just ready to get back to the base."

"I understand, Captain and if everything checks out, we'll have you out of here soon enough."

Brady's frustration was not eased during the next four hours of poking, prodding, and testing but he knew that he was just that much closer to going home.

"We still have a couple of more tests for you," said Dr. Decipeda. "But we need to do those after you get some food in you. I'd think that we're looking at another four hours and then you should be done."

As Brady picked up his food, the doctor stayed in the room.

"You know I went to State also. Quite a few years before you got there and started slinging that pigskin all over the place. I've always been a huge football fan."

"Really. I didn't even know State had a med school. I was good at school but not a doctor or scientist type smart."

The Doctor

"No, I came out here to Stanford for med school."

"That's fitting since their mascot is a tree and now, you're a doctor at a hospital named after a tree."

"Yeah, funny how things work out sometimes. My career started pretty well. I won't bore you with all the details or my resume, but I rose in the ranks pretty quickly. Guess it'd be similar to your career from what I understand. I was actually at Walter Reed and was part of a team of doctors that would examine cabinet members and even the President."

"Wow. What made you decide to come back to the West Coast and work with us common folks?"

"Don't get me wrong. This is a great hospital and I love it here, but it wasn't my choice to leave Walter Reed."

The conversation was interrupted for a few brief moments as a nurse came into the room to get a few signatures from Dr. Decipeda.

But Brady was curious about this friendly doctor.

"You must have made a big mistake, or you made the wrong person mad."

"One of the nurses I supervised made the mistake. Fortunately, nobody died but it was a doozy, nonetheless."

"Then she should have been fired. Are you telling me that you got fired for a mistake somebody else made?"

"It's quite ironic that we just got interrupted by that nurse who wanted my signature a few minutes ago because that is what happened at Walter Reed. You may have noticed, I spent a few extra moments looking the forms over so that I knew what I was signing, and everything looked legit."

"A few years ago, I was working with an individual fresh out of nursing school," said Dr. Decipeda. "I knew better but hurried her through the training. Essentially, I didn't equip her to do her job as well as I should have done."

Brady watched as the doctor checked the monitor and wrote a few numbers on his chart.

Dr. Decipeda continued, "She got some forms mixed up, typed the wrong things, and I signed them. I wish I could say that I trusted her that much, but I was just a little too confident in my abilities and I was also in too big of a hurry that day. When the mistake was discovered, I had two choices: throw her under the bus; or two, take responsibility for my actions. So, here I am."

"Wait, I don't understand," said Brady. "I hope she got fired too. How could you take the blame for that?"

"She was not fired because I resigned," said Dr. Decipeda. "I took responsibility for the mix-up."

Brady was confused by what he was hearing from this doctor.

"Seriously?!? For a smart guy, that wasn't a very smart move. I'd have kicked her to the curb since it wouldn't have been my fault."

"You're right on one thing, Captain Thomas," replied Dr. Decipeda. "If we're playing the blame game, then it's not my fault. But I wasn't just her boss. I wasn't just her supervisor. I wasn't just the person in charge. I was the leader. Being a leader is more than just a title or position."

Dr. Decipeda paused before finishing his story.

"It might not have been my fault," said Dr. Decipeda. "But it was 100% my responsibility to equip her, train her, and help her be the best she possibly could in doing her job. I failed in that responsibility. I didn't equip her properly but then I didn't care enough to coach her up or train her daily or whatever you want to call it."

"I don't know what to say after that," Brady said. "That was a big sacrifice, Doc. I'm just glad you learned your lesson and signed off on the right meds for me."

Brady and Dr. Decipeda shared a chuckle. Brady liked the doctor but couldn't believe what he just heard. That was quite the story.

Now with the doctor gone, Brady turned his attention to the TV. It was obvious the holiday season was just around the corner since the only thing that seemed to be on the screen was the news, shopping networks, or Christmas movies.

WHITE CHRISTMAS

The cafeteria at Laurel Hudson retirement community was festive and spirits were high as some of State's players delivered presents, State swag, and general goodwill to the residents.

The same movie was playing on the television monitor in each corner. *White Christmas* was certainly an old movie but still had some entertaining parts even for college kids.

"We ate, and then he ate. We slept and then he slept."

As the Bing Crosby and Danny Kaye characters talked with respect and admiration for General Waverly on the TV, Lance Prater gently punched Brady in the arm and then pointed up to the TV.

"If you were the general, I'm pretty sure they wouldn't have said the same thing about you," Lance said with a smile. "That's right. Our General, Brady Thomas. We ate ... but only after we got food for him. He was definitely going to eat first. Yep, that's when we ate...after our ..."

Lance paused, cleared his throat with a fake cough, and then finished his statement with the word, "leader."

"Funny guy!" said Brady. "At least you recognize that I'd be a general and in charge of you."

"No matter what you were, I'm sure it'd be prestigious, and you'd find a way to have the corporals carry your bag, briefcase, or even carry 'Your Majesty'."

"Whatever, man."

Just then Coach Casey's voice resonated through the cafeteria.

"Okay, guys. Time to pack up and get back to school for your afternoon meetings and workouts."

"Go ahead and grab the bags, please. I've got to meet with the director, and then I'll see you guys outside on the bus in five minutes."

Almost in unison the guys looked at each other and then looked at the three large duffel bags of State swag and undelivered presents.

It was like they were doing mental math.

Seven guys. Three bags.

It seemed like forever that they stood around not making a move. They were all smart enough to know there were more of them than bags to carry so if they were slow to reach for one, they wouldn't get stuck carrying one out to the bus.

The awkward silence was broken by Jaylen VanVleet, a junior offensive lineman.

"What are we 11 years old?" And with that Jaylen grabbed two of the bags and headed out the door.

One of the freshmen linemen then picked up the other bag and followed closely behind.

"Guess it worked," Brady whispered to his teammate next to him with a smile and then started to leave.

He didn't make it very far before he was interrupted.

"You know, young man," one of the residents said to Brady on the way out. "Those bags aren't very heavy for strong guys like you. Don't think for an instance I didn't see what you guys did over there. I just hope that you react quicker to a fumble than you did to your coach's instructions to grab the bags."

Brady barely even comprehended that he was just lectured by some old dude. But the only appropriate comeback Brady could utter at that moment was, "Yes sir."

Brady walked to the bus a little shell shocked at what just happened. Didn't that old guy know who he was talking to?

"Hey Brady, y'all have fun?"

Speaking of older gentlemen. No matter what was going on in Brady's mind, Mr. Frank always seemed to bring a smile to his face.

"Absolutely. What isn't there to like about taking time out of our already busy schedule to go to an old folk's home. No offense, though Mr. Frank." Brady said with a smile and a hint of sarcasm as he greeted the team's bus driver with a high five.

GUARD DOG

Brady took his seat a few rows behind the bus driver.

"I hear you met the old Guard Dog?" said Mr. Frank.

Brady seemed confused.

"Old Guard Dog?"

"Well, that was his nickname, but his real name was Tom Mariner."

"I'm not sure? We met a lot of old people today. Which one was he?" Brady asked.

"He was the guy that cornered you just a few minutes ago and grilled you about picking up those bags."

"Oh, yeah that guy. It was a little weird. It's not that big of a deal. I don't know why he even wasted his time with something like that. He might not know who I am but if he did, he'd probably understand I don't need to be carrying bags, especially when there are other guys around. But really, I didn't think much of it honestly."

"You probably should have," said Mr. Frank. "He might not have known who you were, but I'm guessing you have no idea who he is either."

"Just some old 'get off my lawn' type dude, probably."

"That could well be true," Mr. Frank agreed. "But that old Guard Dog Tom Mariner is someone you should know. He's had quite the life. He was named an All-American halfback three different times way back in the day when they didn't wear facemasks. He was one tough guy."

Mr. Frank continued his story as he pulled the bus out of the parking lot of the retirement community.

"Not only was he hard to bring down when he was carrying the pigskin, but he also blocked guys and protected his quarterback like an offensive lineman. Lots of people thought his nickname was the Junkyard Dog because he was so tough, but it was Guard Dog because he looked out for his guys – his teammates."

"That carried over into the military. He eventually was a TOPGUN pilot."

That got Brady's attention. He'd lost track of how many times he'd watched that movie growing up. It was one of the few non-football-related things he and his dad would watch together.

"Old Guard Dog even got a medal back in the war. One of his guys was shot down behind enemy lines and he purposely crash-landed his plane to be with his buddy. Together they eluded the enemy and avoided capture for a week until they were able to be rescued. In other words, the guy you ran into a few minutes ago knows a little something about being a winner. He was quite the hero. Talk about a real leader. Yes sir, old Tom Mariner. That old Guard Dog was something."

Brady had always respected the team's bus driver. The young quarterback appreciated the encouraging words Mr. Frank offered the guys. It seemed the coaches also had a fondness for Mr. Frank and treated him like he was part of the staff.

It seemed everyone listened to Mr. Frank when he had the wisdom to impart or stories to tell. Brady was no exception, though he did find himself rolling his eyes once or twice as any college student would when an older person was giving any "back in my day" speeches.

HEAVY LIFTING

The bus was still ten minutes from campus when Mr. Frank broke the silence.

"Hey Brady, care to humor an old man with one more story?"

"Do I have a choice when it comes to another episode of storytime with Mr. Frank?" Brady said with a huge grin.

"You could always just pretend you're listening to some of that noise on your headphones," Mr. Frank said while matching Brady's grin.

"Way back in the day during the American Revolutionary War," Mr. Frank began. "A rider on horseback came across a group of soldiers under the command of a corporal who was out to show he was in charge. The soldiers were moving timber trying to build a wall alongside a road. This corporal kept barking out orders because remember, he was in charge. He was the boss.

Mr. Frank continued with his story, "Despite trying with all their might to push the final log in place up top, they just couldn't do it. Every time the last log would come crashing down and the corporal would yell louder."

"Sounds like they needed to get swole. They needed to get into the weight room," joked Brady.

"Yep, if only they had some squat racks in their weight rooms back in 1775," replied Mr. Frank with a smile. "Anyway, remember I started off saying there was this guy on a horse. Well, he got off and

Heavy Lifting

went over to the soldiers. This guy took his place alongside them, inspiring them to lift as one unit and that big old log slid right into place."

"That's what I'm talking about," Brady said. "That dude didn't mess around."

"You're right Brady," said Mr. Frank. "But just as quickly as he joined the men, this stranger got back up on his horse looking to be on his way. The corporal ran over to him and thanked him for adding a little extra muscle to the job. The man asked the corporal why he hadn't helped his men with the heavy lifting. Brady, do you know what that corporal said?"

Brady shook his head. He knew Mr. Frank was getting close to the end of the story, which always seemed to have a point. Brady didn't know how that corporal was going to respond.

Mr. Frank continued, "The corporal reminded the stranger of his rank, and that heavy lifting wasn't done by the person in charge."

"That kind of makes sense," Brady said. "He'd probably paid his dues and earned that right."

"Well, speaking of paying dues," Mr. Frank responded. "That stranger told the corporal to call upon him the next time there was some heavy lifting required. He then opened his coat revealing a fancy uniform and introduced himself to the corporal. Before galloping away, General George Washington made it clear that he was willing to help out if the corporal encountered something else that was beneath his title and position. He would help with the heavy lifting."

"Okay, didn't see that one coming," said Brady. "Thanks for the history lesson, Mr. Frank."

"We can learn valuable lessons anytime, like from your all-conference left tackle, Jaylen. The guy who protects your blindside wasn't above grabbing a bag today. He grabbed two of the three bags. He has status. He has seniority. But it didn't matter. He wasn't too good to do the heavy lifting, just like our first president, George Washington."

Brady couldn't help but take a quick look at Jaylen a few seats farther back in the bus. It was kind of weird that Jaylen was so quick to pick up those bags. Mr. Frank might be on to something, and he wasn't quite finished, either.

"Dr. Martin Luther King used to say everybody can be great because anybody can serve. Serving doesn't mean you're inferior. It just means that you're helpful and useful. The best leaders earn respect not just by excelling on the field of competition, but by constantly helping the people around them."

Brady smiled as Mr. Frank gathered momentum.

"You can't be a real leader unless you're willing to serve those around you," Mr. Frank said. "Real leaders are not worried about titles, positions, status, or power. Real leadership isn't about barking orders but rather about helping others to do the heavy lifting. George Washington was more concerned about helping and serving than he was concerned about his rank, uniform, or power that he had."

Just then there was a voice from behind Brady.

"That's right Mr. Frank. Say it a little louder for the people in the back," said Jaylen. "I feel like it's Sunday morning up here in this bus."

Brady rolled his eyes and chuckled at Jaylen's comment.

"Okay, Mr. Frank. Next time, I'll use my muscles and help that big ol' offensive lineman by carrying a bag or two," Brady said with a smile.

Mr. Frank wasn't sure if Brady had gotten the point of the story but the fact that he'd listened to the story was a positive sign at least.

LEAVING THE HOSPITAL

It seemed like it was a long time ago that he was punching out of his FA-18 leading to a required hospital visit, but now it was finally time to go. Brady had received a clean bill of health – at least physically speaking that is.

Mentally, he was still fixated on the blame game. Dr. Decipeda had an unusual perspective on leadership, taking responsibility, and not worrying about whose fault it was. But that wasn't for Brady.

He grabbed the small go-bag that accompanied him on all his flights and headed out the lobby door.

It would take about an hour to drive back to the base, and he was hoping for some much-needed shut-eye. However, there was probably not much chance of that since his driver would be a blast from the past.

Brady couldn't help but smile when he thought of the friendly and talkative bus driver from his college football days.

Fortunately, Mr. Frank lived relatively close to the hospital and didn't hesitate when Brady called him. He'd been friendly through the years and was always sending a card or a text encouraging Brady.

Mr. Frank had always been that way. Even though the guys would lovingly joke about how he seemed to have a story for every occasion, it was obvious how much he cared about the guys he drove around.

THE CAPTAIN

It didn't surprise Brady that Mr. Frank had all of those stories since he'd lived quite an interesting life. His experiences in the military, being a firefighter, driving 18-wheelers, and serving as a sheriff's deputy, provided a good foundation for Mr. Frank as he offered wisdom to both the coaching staff and State's players.

Rumor had it that he even built his own house and made customized John Deere tractors in his spare time. He was quite fascinating, but the thing Brady liked about him the most was that he didn't want anything from the guys on the team. He was one of the few people Brady had ever interacted with that seemed to be genuine and sincere. Brady certainly like attention and loved all the media coverage of him but something was refreshing about Mr. Frank and how he treated Brady the same win or lose, good game or bad game.

As Brady waited for his ride, memories of his only other hospital stay crept into his mind.

Ironically, Mr. Frank had picked him up that day as well.

PHILLY SPECIAL

Even though Brady had been knocked out on national television, he was only in the hospital overnight. All of his teammates had left to go back to campus for classes and meetings.

Coach Casey had arranged for Mr. Frank to bring Brady back to campus.

Brady got up from the lobby sofa as he saw Mr. Frank enter.

"Hey Brady, sorry about the game and your injury, but I'm really glad you're okay. It didn't look good."

"Thanks, Mr. Frank," replied Brady. "It didn't feel too good either. Was rough. My head is still throbbing, but I'll be back before you know it."

"Coach said he has people already scheduled to regularly check in on you. You aren't supposed to be alone when you get a concussion."

"I guess. It's never happened to me before. It's kind of a weird feeling."

"Back in my day, there were no concussions," said Mr. Frank. "We just got our bell rung so to speak. I wish we had the medical advances and the science like you guys do now. I can't imagine all the ways we harmed our bodies back then trying to be macho or just not knowing things."

Mr. Frank picked up Brady's bag and together they walked to the car.

"That new kid, John Tyna, really had a rough go of it today when you went out. I hear he is very talented and has a bright future. When you get to feeling better, you might want to say something to him. I'm guessing you'll be out for a few more games."

"One game tops!" Brady said with conviction. "I'm not letting those trainers keep me out any longer than some stupid protocol says."

"Well, I don't know about all that. But as long as you're on the sideline whether it's in practice or a game, that Tyna kid is going to be running the show. He probably needs a little encouragement. I bet it would mean a lot coming from you."

Brady had no reply to Mr. Frank. He didn't necessarily agree or disagree with what Mr. Frank had just said. Brady wasn't in much of a mood to encourage others.

After a few minutes of driving, Brady was still awake, so Mr. Frank broke the silence.

"Hey Brady, do you remember Super Bowl 52 when the Eagles won?"

"Yes sir! How could I forget that game? The quarterback catching a touchdown pass."

"I figured you'd remember that being a quarterback," laughed Mr. Frank.

"Absolutely. I remember that the Eagles were huge underdogs, and that 'Philly Special' play beat the Patriots. I wish Coach Casey would put that play in the offense. I'd love to catch a touchdown pass."

"That would be pretty exciting," responded Mr. Frank. "I will never forget that game because it was the culmination of an interesting season for the Eagles. Carson Wentz was their quarterback, and he was the odds-on favorite to win the league MVP award but then he tore his ACL in Week 14."

Mr. Frank continued, "Nick Foles was the backup but, in the NFL, probably like on your team, the backup doesn't get many reps with the starters. But Foles comes in and helps them win that Week 14 game and then he wins two of the last three regular-season games as a starter. He wins all three playoff games, as well. Foles and Wentz were friends and encouraged one another. Wentz helped prepare Foles during the season just in case."

Brady could always recall the Philly Special and Nick Foles winning Super Bowl MVP, but he'd forgotten the backstory until Mr. Frank refreshed his memory.

"Carson Wentz wanted his team to be great," said Mr. Frank. "He understood that he was the franchise quarterback and so he probably wasn't scared of Nick Foles. But he probably also understood that football is a physical sport and that if Foles ever had to step into that role, he needed to be prepared. I'm guessing they don't win the Super Bowl that year if Foles and Wentz are adversaries and jealous of one another."

"Well, if John and I ever make it to the NFL and play on the same team one day, I will encourage him so that he can be a great backup … during my MVP season," Brady said.

Mr. Frank smiled as he saw the big grin on Brady's face in the rear-view mirror.

BACK ON BASE

It seemed like Déjà vu all over again.
Brady was walking out of a hospital and getting a ride home from Mr. Frank.

After the two embraced, they headed to the black SUV to make the trip back to the Naval Air Station.

Brady figured Mr. Frank would probably have a story to tell, but he also knew that the old bus driver had a lot of wisdom and would understand Brady was not in the mood to talk.

Surprisingly it was Brady that broke the silence once the SUV hit the highway.

"Thanks so much for picking me up on such short notice. It's great that you live so close and were available."

"You're very welcome, Brady," said Mr. Frank. "Happy to help you out. What a scare. Nobody likes having to go to the hospital. I'm just so thankful that you're okay. No broken bones or anything wrong physically, right?"

"Yep. I was in the hospital for a minute, but it was just routine. I'm fine physically. Nothing hurts. I'm fine. Can't say the same for my plane, or the guy that messed up on the preflight check."

"Oh, what happened to that guy?"

"Nothing YET!" Brady said. "But I'm going to find him when I get back to base."

"You sound angry, Brady."

"Yeah, I'm ticked but I'm mostly exaggerating as to what I'd do. I'm smart enough to know that my career is more important than messing' up this guy."

"That's good to hear. I was a little concerned there for a moment. What did happen if you don't mind me asking?"

"It was weird," Brady said as he recalled the events that led to his ejection. One minute everything is normal and the next it's like I'm in a movie. Fortunately, all my training kicked in and I ended up okay."

"I'm so glad to hear that. I know that flying is easy for you. It's like driving a car for the rest of us, but there is still always that element of danger. I'm just glad you're okay."

"Thanks, Mr. Frank. I appreciate it."

"I hope you find some answers, Brady," said Mr. Frank. "I also hope that you keep your composure. Just remember not to make one problem worse by creating another problem. Also, just remember the lesson from that old pirate movie you guys used to watch on the bus."

"Pirates of the Caribbean," Brady recalled. "Great movie but what was that lesson. Don't mess with pirate ghosts or don't mess with Jack Sparrow?"

"Neither. There is a part in the movie when Captain Jack Sparrow says that the problem is not the problem. The problem is your attitude toward the problem. Great advice for all of us to remember."

"Yes sir. How can I argue with such a true and noble historical figure like Captain Jack Sparrow?" Brady joked.

The two of them drove in silence for the next few minutes as Brady slowly fell asleep.

After a 45-minute power nap, the SUV arrived on base. The two old friends said their goodbyes and the black SUV rolled away as Brady unlocked his front door.

THE CAPTAIN

The on-base home was a sight for sore eyes as he kicked off his shoes and plopped down on his sofa. Within minutes, he was fast asleep. Brady had underestimated how tired he was.

His personal investigation into the incident would have to wait a little while longer.

He hadn't taken the time to ponder what the last day had meant in his life. He wasn't very introspective. Since 2013, more than 200 military pilots or aircrew had been killed in aviation mishaps. He was lucky.

Brady never gave much thought to his weaknesses or how lucky he was or wasn't. He knew his abilities. He'd always been talented. He'd always been hard working. He'd always believed that you get what you deserve.

His success was due to what he did or didn't do. As far as he was concerned, there was a problem that caused him to punch out. That problem – or failure – was someone else's fault. The solution – his successful ejection and rescue – was because of his ability to react properly.

He might be part of a team, but he was the pilot. He was the captain. He was the star of that team. The role players were replaceable and if they weren't going to do their jobs right then we'd need to get others in their place. The rest of the team needs to make sure that they're not making it tough on the fighter pilot. After all, without a fighter pilot, there would be no need for aircraft maintenance workers.

Soon it would be time for Brady to get to the bottom of just why somebody's incompetence nearly killed him.

MEETING WITH GRAND

Andy Grand had been the commander of the Air Wing Carrier Division before Brady but was now the Admiral for the Carrier Strike Group. Brady was not only envious of the one-star Admiral and his position of leadership but also the fact that he'd been an instructor at TOPGUN. Brady liked him but had always wondered why, with all of Admiral Grand's connections, he was not able to pull strings to get Brady into TOPGUN.

"Come in Brady," Admiral Grand said as he motioned Brady to a seat. "Welcome back. I'm glad that you're okay. We train and prepare but hope to never have to use our skills in that way."

"Yes sir. Thank you."

"We wanted to give you an extra day to get some additional rest and get acclimated back to base life. I know you weren't gone very long but it was a still traumatic event."

Brady waited for the Admiral to continue and get to the punchline. He wanted to hear whose fault this was and why he was forced to be in such a traumatic event, as he said.

"I also wanted to give you an update on how things will be unfolding as we move forward. As you know an official investigation has begun. Our preliminary findings have been inconclusive in finding the cause of the accident. We're presently salvaging the plane, or rather what's left of it. Fortunately for us, the weather has been cooperative the last 24 hours and looks like it will stay that way for the next few days."

Surely, Admiral Grand would give Brady some nugget of hope in determining whose fault this had been.

"We're combing over all the data and computer information we have," Admiral Grand continued. "We have also conducted preliminary interviews with everyone associated with your plane. This includes the immediate debrief we had with you at the hospital just to make sure there wasn't something obvious or urgent that we needed to know. You're scheduled for a more in-depth session tomorrow. However, as of right now, we don't have any conclusive findings. We're early in the process, but I wanted to still give you an update."

"Thank you, sir," was all Brady could muster at the moment.

Brady left the office unsure of how he should feel about the whole thing.

Maintenance logs were now computerized. Even though it had only been a couple of days, surely, they would have found something by now.

Just like the Navy's investigation wasn't complete, neither was Brady's. His unofficial detective work still had a few more stones to turn over.

REDWOOD TREES

It had been nearly three days since Mr. Frank had dropped Brady off at his house. Brady couldn't think of anyone better to call to get some perspective on his situation.

"Oh Brady, it's so good to hear from you. I know how busy you must be. How is your investigation going?"

"I talked to all of the guys that had anything to do with my plane before takeoff and none of them would admit to any errors. It was really strange. Nothing seemed off in the logs either."

"Well, what does all that mean Brady?" asked Mr. Frank.

"I'm not sure. I'm a little confused, to be honest. I was doing my best detective bit, while also throwing around my weight a bit, and still, I couldn't get any of them to crack."

"Were you expecting a confession?"

He couldn't see him, but Brady was pretty sure the old bus driver was probably smirking a little bit on the other end of the phone.

"I'm not sure exactly, but I did figure on finding out what went wrong. But it just got weirder from there."

"How so, Brady?"

"Even though I wasn't at Sequoia very long, they began a preliminary investigation here without me."

"Sequoia? That was the hospital I picked you up from, right? Our family has always gone to the other hospital in that area."

"Yep. I guess Sequoia is kind of a big deal in the region. Lots of important people go there for their procedures. They're always having huge charity events."

"I'm not a big deal so maybe that's why I don't go there," remarked Mr. Frank. "I do like those sequoia redwood trees, though. They're huge. They are a big deal, my friend."

It seemed like forever that there was silence over the phone, but it was only a second or two. Brady had heard Mr. Frank say things like this in the past. Statements like he just made were normally followed by some sort of sage advice or story.

Brady was right. This time was no exception.

"Redwood trees are the tallest in the world. I'm sure you've seen a bunch of them during your time on the West Coast."

Mr. Frank continued, "They're hundreds of feet tall but what most people don't know is their roots are not very deep. Very tall trees with narrow roots are not a good combination."

"No, it doesn't sound like it. I'd think they would fall over easily," Brady said.

Mr. Frank shook his head in agreement.

"Yes, that would make sense, but their root system spreads out hundreds of feet underground. Instead of being deep, they are wide. As those roots spread out, they get mixed up with the roots from their neighbors."

"These trees support one another, not only from the elements but also in sharing water and other nutrients crucial to survival. Essentially, this is the same with a team."

Mr. Frank continued with that though, "To have a strong team, you must support one another. Each member needs to hold each other up, work together and share in each other's strengths as you hide each other's weaknesses. The Redwoods are the biggest trees in the world, but they need their neighbors, their teammates, to help them survive and thrive."

"I guess it makes sense, in theory," said Brady. "When I played at State, my offensive linemen were supposed to protect me. My wide receivers were supposed to run good routes and catch my passes. If they didn't do their part, then my passes would have been incomplete."

"But that is only part of it," responded Mr. Frank. "Speaking of trees and sliding a little cheesiness into this conversation, you have to see the whole forest and not just your tree. Teamwork isn't just a one-way street. Teamwork isn't just role players or others working for the stars. Great teams have great teammates. Just like all the sequoia redwoods have to work together to keep each other from falling, so it is with a team. Everyone works together to accomplish things they probably couldn't have done on their own. No matter your role or status, you should always be figuring out how you can support or make your teammates better."

"That also kind of makes this whole situation with your plane interesting. In hearing you talk, it sounds like you're part of a team once again just like you were at State. You obviously can't do it alone because you rely on others to do maintenance or whatever it is you guys do with your planes."

Brady wasn't excited about talk of teamwork but what Mr. Frank was saying made sense. Surprisingly, Brady didn't automatically reject it and get defensive.

"The best teams grow together," said Mr. Frank. "They celebrate successes together. They overcome challenges together. This mentality and attitude are contagious and can quickly spread. Pretty soon the whole team is acting as one. They're doing what's best for the entire team, not just themselves or their position. With a football team, it's no longer 'the wide receivers cost us the game' or 'we would have won if the defense had done their job'. With the Navy, I'm sure it's similar. Collective responsibility ... everybody is responsible for each other. Kind of like those sequoias."

THE CAPTAIN

Of course, teamwork was a concept all of Brady's coaches emphasized repeatedly, but they had never framed it the way Mr. Frank had just done.

Regardless, Brady still had some work to do to find out what happened with his plane, and he needed to jump off the call but wanted to tell Mr. Frank one last thing.

"Good stuff," said Brady. "But before you started that story, I meant to tell you. Early in the investigation, nobody could find anything the crew did wrong precheck. Nobody can figure out what happened."

"The main thing is that you're safe," said Mr. Frank. "I'm sure you guys will figure it out. I hope that it isn't anyone's fault if that is possible. It's tough for a team to be successful when team members are playing the blame game."

As they said their good-byes, Brady couldn't help but think about that blame game comment and how it played into his situation.

COACH CASEY HONORED

It was somewhat unusual for a former star athlete, but Brady had only been back to campus once since he'd graduated. There had never been a good reason to make the trip since he was busy with his career.

Today was different. Coach Casey was being inducted into the school's hall of honor. He'd just finished up another great season winning ten games including a Rose Bowl victory. The school would recognize him at halftime of the basketball game and then host a fabulous banquet in his honor. He'd already announced that next season would be his last, but the school didn't want to hold off on this well-deserved recognition.

It'd been nearly two months since his incident, and he'd yet to find the person or the reason that caused the malfunction. All indications were the Review Board was in the final stages of their investigation and the report would soon be finished.

The banquet was a good distraction from what was going on in Brady's life.

There were at least 200 former players at the banquet, which was a small testament to Coach Casey's popularity. Afterward, there was a special small gathering for Coach Casey's family, former staff, and past All-Americans. It was a much more intimate setting.

Toward the end of the evening, Brady found himself talking with John Tyna, his former backup turned NFL star and Coach Casey.

"I think back on those days and there was some star power in that quarterback meeting room," remembered Coach Casey. "A Heisman Trophy winner who'd one day be a war hero and another guy that would end up being an NFL star. You don't see that every day."

"Pretty impressive indeed," John agreed. "I learned a lot from those meetings and that year we were together. I don't think I'd have had anywhere close to the career I've had if not for that year and getting to know Brady."

The two former teammates had kept in touch over the years but never really shared intimate thoughts and feelings. John's sentiment caught Brady a little off balance.

"Yeah, you learned what not to do," joked Brady. "You made it and I didn't. Not sure there was much I taught you on being an NFL quarterback."

"Your work ethic was incredible, Brady," Coach Casey pointed out.

"I don't mean for you to take this the wrong way man," started John. "But some of the things you did as a teammate and leader were not necessarily helpful to me on the surface. But you were the first person I ever met that was an awesome player, who worked hard but didn't necessarily take the time to make his teammates better."

"Wow, thanks for not sugarcoating it, John!"

"We all have to grow and learn," John said. "I wanted to be you. Athlete Brady. Star Brady. Captain Brady. But I soon realized that if I was like the teammate Brady, I'd never fulfilled my potential or help my teammates achieve their potential as well."

John continued, "We all learn. You didn't necessarily have anyone to learn from until you got into the Navy. Now, look at you. Man, everything looks great for you. I'm happy for you."

Brady took a big breath as he digested all of this. John had no idea what Brady had really been going through the last couple of months.

He certainly had no idea that Brady hadn't changed much from his playing days.

"Good things can come from bad situations," John Continued. "An injury occurs and maybe a different player gets to develop more. A tragedy occurs and people come together and unify. Someone has a mild heart attack and it's the wake-up call they need to lose some weight. You didn't do everything right as a leader when you were in college, but I learned from that and have had a positive influence on so many more people than I'd have otherwise."

Everything John was saying was true and made sense to Brady, but it didn't mean he was enjoying it. However, it brought something else to mind that had been bothering him for quite some time.

"Coach, when they were going over all your accomplishments and stuff at the banquet, they said something that kind of surprised me and I wanted to ask you about it," Brady inquired.

"They said a lot of things but don't believe half of it," Coach said with a sly smile. "At least that's what my wife always says. Those weeds aren't going to pick themselves. The grass doesn't care what your bowl record is. She always sets me straight."

"Oh, I believe it, Coach. That sounds just like Miss Brenda," Brady said. "At the banquet, the guy said that 32 of your 33 graduating classes had either won a bowl game or a conference title at some point during their four years at State."

Brady paused for a moment but the look on Coach's face told him that he knew where he was going next.

"I never won a bowl game or conference title while I was at State," Brady said. "My class was the group that kept you from having a perfect record."

"It's not about my record Brady," Coach said. "I was always just sad that we couldn't have helped you guys better and made that possible."

THE CAPTAIN

"But I was the quarterback. I won a Heisman for Pete's sake! How could we have lost so much? Was that my fault since I was the quarterback? I feel like I should be apologizing."

"No need to apologize Brady. I can tell you that it wasn't your fault any more than it was Jaylen's fault or John's fault or Lance's fault. Football is a team sport. Shoot, life is a team sport. What one person does affects others. So many things go into losing so it's hard to point a finger at one person or one thing. Just like winning. When you'd pass for 300 yards and four touchdowns, you weren't the sole reason that we won. You didn't catch your own passes. You didn't block for yourself. You didn't make any tackles. In the same way, when you had a bad game, it wasn't your fault we lost."

"I appreciate you saying it wasn't my fault, but it still seems strange that I was so successful, yet the team wasn't," Brady lamented. "Especially considering all your other teams were good. Plus, you said that you always felt bad about our class, but it definitely wasn't your fault."

Coach Casey shook his head looking at both John and Brady.

"Finding fault is such a short-term and short-sighted approach to life. Negativity or playing the blame game rarely leads you to anyplace good in life. It might feel good at the moment. At the end of the day, it was my responsibility to maximize the strengths and success of every team and every athlete I coached. It was my responsibility to help you be a better quarterback but also to be a better leader. It was my responsibility to help all 100 of you guys come together and be the best team possible. It was on me to find ways to make that happen."

John had been listening and taking in all of the conversations and wanted to try and put a nice little bow around it before he had to leave.

"That is part of being a real leader. Brady, you've probably seen that in the military. Win or lose together. Succeed or fail in the mission together. Everyone has each other's backs. Learning from the past so that you have a better future. That is kind of what I was talking about earlier. I saw some of the ways you as a 22-year old acted and realized I was heading down that same road as a leader. I became better because of you."

"Well, since I made you who you are today little brother, how about you cut me in on some of that big contract extension you just signed, huh?" Brady joked.

"Oh, would you look at the time?" a grinning John said as he tapped his watch and started to put on his coat.

REVIEW BOARD

Brady took his seat in front of the review board. Because this was a Class-A accident, a three-star Admiral was the presiding officer.

Admiral Null was well-respected and took the lead in communicating the board's findings. She'd served on the USS Rushmore in the last 1990s when Michelle Howard became the first African American to command a naval ship. Howard would go on to become the first woman to earn the rank of four-star admiral in the U.S. Navy. She was Admiral Null's mentor.

"We have received the investigation results. We'll be discussing them and informing you of the course of action moving forward."

"Yes, ma'am."

"A thorough review has taken place," Admiral Null said. "During the last two months since the incident in question, all relevant flight and maintenance logs, wreckage, black box recordings, statements from relevant personnel, and computer data have been examined. It's the findings of this board the crash was caused by pilot error."

Brady couldn't maintain his poker face when he heard the phrase pilot error. He was confused.

"All findings are documented in precise detail in the report in front of you. In simple terms, this extremely unfortunate incident occurred because your engine didn't get enough fuel."

"Fuel? All due respect, ma'am, I had plenty of fuel. It was a routine training flight."

"You're correct, Captain. You did have adequate fuel; however, the wing intake switch was in the off position. None of the fuel in your wings made it to the engine. When the main compartment ran out, the engine no longer received any fuel. Captain, you essentially ran out of gas."

"Ma'am, there has to be more to it.?" Brady asked in confusion.

"I agree but pilot error is what our report concludes. There is no proof of malicious intent or deliberate sabotage of your aircraft, nor did your actions lead to loss of life. However, you signed your name to the pre-flight log. You either overlooked the wing intake switch or disengaged it during flight."

Admiral Null continued, "Captain Thomas, I know that you have been adamant since the accident that it wasn't your fault. You have stated multiple times you have no idea what happened. However, it's the board's conclusion the events of that routine training flight were avoidable, and you were the only person that could have prevented this situation. Before I go any further, do you have any questions or need clarification on these findings?"

"No ma'am," Brady stated. "I still don't fully understand why or how this happened. But I do understand after talking with other people and thinking about the situation that nobody else could have prevented this more than me. I came in here today not knowing the final outcome of the investigation. Certainly, I had hoped and believed it wasn't my fault, but my own inquiries revealed I also couldn't logically pin this on anyone else. It had to be either someone's fault or just an unfortunate accident that could not have been prevented. We know now that it could have been prevented and someone has to be held accountable. I'm that person."

"That is not quite the response I was expecting, Captain," Admiral Null said in surprise.

Brady was not shocked by this statement. He was fully aware that he didn't have the reputation of someone who admits when he is wrong.

"You have a history of doing things your own way and having a certain opinion of yourself that others might not share."

"Yes, ma'am. I understand," agreed Brady. "So, what happens next?"

"Your next sea deployment is not for another six months," Admiral Null said. "You'll be officially grounded for the next 60 days, during which time you will be assessed for basic aviator protocols. After that, you'll be able to get back up in the sky on a probationary period for an additional 60 days. Make no mistake, starting now you're on a short leash and will have to prove that you're not only a team player, but have learned from this incident. Mistakes of this nature are expensive, life-threatening, and can be career-ending. However, the more important aspect of this situation is taking accountability and understanding that blaming others for your actions is detrimental to the team."

BRADY'S REQUEST

Brady sat there for a moment processing what he'd just heard. There was something on his mind and he felt he needed to say it.

"Permission to speak freely, ma'am?" Brady asked.

"Yes but realize that our decision is final."

"Yes ma'am," said Brady. "I'm still working through some of these thoughts and processing this whole thing being on my shoulders. You can imagine that it has been a significant blow to my ego."

"You're not used to failure, I understand."

"I'm also not used to evaluating myself critically and admitting mistakes."

"So, what is this request, Captain?"

"Each of you on this review board graduated from TOPGUN. As you know, I've gotten rejected three different times, which has to be some kind of record. I admit I haven't necessarily had a good attitude about this..."

Admiral Null interrupted him. "Captain, I think I see where this is going, and you're in no position to request acceptance into TOPGUN. There are reasons for your application being rejected and that was before you destroyed your aircraft due to pilot error. I think deep down you probably know why you have been and will continue to be rejected, so don't waste any more of your time or our time with this topic."

"No, ma'am. That's not actually what I was going to ask, though I can see why you might have thought that. I know there are several guys here that want to go to TOPGUN. I want to help them. It's too late for me, but I want to provide some direction and also show them some ways that I've messed up my chances over the years. I have not always provided the best example of leadership but maybe others can learn from my mistakes. I'd like your permission to set up a few sessions with other officers, or anyone for that matter, over the next couple of months before my next deployment."

"Interesting. Where did this come from?" Admiral Null asked.

"This might sound kind of silly, but the past two months have like a retelling of a Christmas Carol. I wasn't visited by three ghosts on Christmas Eve like Ebenezer Scrooge was but instead have talked with enough people I respect to realize some things about myself that I don't like. I didn't see my future like Scrooge, but I did have a close call with death. I've had time to think about a lot of things from my career. I know now I've not been a good leader. I can't change my past, but I can start today to be better."

Observing the skepticism on Admiral Null's face, Brady continued, "I know, I know. I can't believe I just said some of that, myself. That's like some Hallmark card or locker room motivational poster."

"Captain Thomas, you say you've not been a good leader, but you're a Navy Cross recipient, Heisman Trophy-winning quarterback, and a captain in the U.S. Navy. How does that mesh? How are you all of those things but you're not a good leader?"

"You're right, ma'am. That doesn't mesh," Brady agreed. "It's always been my goal to get into TOPGUN, but I always thought of it like graduate school or advanced training. I knew it was only available to the best of the best, which I assumed would be me. But the best of the best isn't just about talent. In the last few weeks, I've started learning more about TOPGUN and the character of those who are accepted. You all graduated from there, so this realization is not new to you, but it's new to me as well as the others here that dream of wearing the patch."

Brady continued, "TOPGUN doesn't train aviators to be more talented at flying. It trains them on how to make their squads better. It trains them to make others better. It trains them to train other aviators. It's about the whole team, leaders developing other leaders. Leaders help shape future leaders. I'm perhaps stating the obvious to those of you in this room."

Brady paused for a moment wondering if Admiral Null would say something, either good or bad. But the Admiral wanted to see if Brady had more to say. This was a little unusual and he didn't want to interrupt Brady's flow.

"I believed that I earned my ranks. I earned my status. I earned my positions. But recently, I have realized that I never earned the right to lead others. My career is full of achieving my goals and my desires, but I never helped others achieve theirs. A good leader takes people from where they are to where they want to be. I have never considered other's goals, just mine."

"I'm saying all of this as if I've figured it all out. Intellectually, it makes sense to me now, but I'm going to struggle to execute it. I have 20 years of bad habits, but that doesn't mean I can't start now. It doesn't mean that I can't pass on some of the lessons I've learned or use some of my experiences to others."

Brady took a sip of water from the glass in front of him as he awaited a response from Admiral Null.

"I must admit I'm surprised by what you're saying, and relieved to finally hear it," said Admiral Null. "I'd agree that you haven't maximized your natural leadership qualities. You have a lot of charisma, intelligence, a tremendous work ethic, talent, and an ability to quickly learn. With all that said, it appears you've also always been missing something – an understanding of what real leadership is. I'm glad you're starting to realize your shortcomings. However, nothing you said changes the findings in the report or the consequences. We'll consider your request to work with other aviators to teach them some lessons that you've learned."

"Yes, ma'am. It's not easy to hear that I'm responsible for the accident. I wasn't sure about the result of this meeting. I was hoping for a different outcome, but over the last few weeks and months, I've started to understand what REAL leadership looks like."

"And what is that Captain?" asked Admiral Null.

"Real leaders are responsible, empower others, are able to connect with others, and lead by example. I'm afraid I've fallen short in this area. Leadership isn't just about a person's status, talent, or position."

SURPRISE LETTER

Brady barely waited for Admiral Grand to acknowledge the knock on his door.

"Did you know about this?" asked Brady as he stepped into the office waving the letter in the air.

Though Brady's suspension had ended, and he was back in the cockpit, things were not 'back to normal'. Brady was still the same talented pilot he always was, but there was something different about him as a leader.

The lessons he'd mentioned to the review board ended up being real to him after all. There was some skepticism that he'd said what he had in an attempt to avoid disciplinary action. However, his actions in the months since had confirmed that he'd changed his views on what leadership meant.

Not only was he diligent in meeting regularly with Admiral Grand, but his attitude was markedly changed from what it was in the past when they met. Brady saw every meeting as another opportunity to develop and become a better leader. It wasn't just an inconvenience or obligation on his calendar, these meetings were valuable to his continued growth. As he improved and learned, then he could, in turn, help his guys become better.

Brady enthusiastically slapped the letter down on the desk and Admiral Grand began to read,

THE CAPTAIN

Captain Thomas,
Thank you for applying for the TOPGUN program. As you know, there are limited spots available in each class. Candidates are evaluated, not only on their competency and ability, but also their demonstrated leadership qualities and their ability to work within a team. After careful consideration, we're extending an offer to join us in the next class at TOPGUN. Congratulations on this first step in becoming a TOPGUN pilot. We look forward to having you in Nevada.

"Well, I guess congrats are in order for you," said Admiral Grand.

"Thank you, sir," responded Brady. "But you didn't answer my initial question. Did you know this?"

"Yes. I talked with a number of my friends at Fallon. You've been rejected many times in the past. It was never because of your talent. It was always because they didn't trust that you'd be a good teammate. They didn't quite believe that when push came to shove that you'd be a leader they could be proud of."

Admiral Grand handed the letter back to Brady.

"I can't tell you how proud I am of you," he said. "We're going to miss you because you're just starting to get it. The potential you have moving forward to positively impact others is unlimited. When the most talented person on a team is also the best leader and teammate, then great things can be accomplished."

Brady was truly moved and humbled at what his mentor and superior officer was saying.

"Thank you, sir. I won't let you down. I will make you proud."

"You already have made me proud in the way you've grown these last few months. I look forward to seeing you become an amazing person of influence moving forward."

The two shook hands and then continued with their regularly scheduled meeting.

There was still much to do at the Naval Air Station before Brady would leave for Fallon. But whether he was at Naval Station Fallon, on deployment aboard an aircraft carrier, or anywhere else, he would continue to be a person of influence. Brady now understood that real leadership wasn't about power, status, titles, or even talent.

The captain who had always been in leadership positions would finally become a REAL leader.

LETTER TO COACH CASEY

Coach Casey, I appreciated your note congratulating me on getting into TOPGUN. The last few months have been crazy, and I've learned so much! I wish I had a time machine and could play for you again at State. I'd be a quarterback that was a REAL leader this time. We'd win championships and bowl games not because I was more talented but because I was the kind of leader the team needed.

I wanted to write you and tell you a few of the things that I've learned in the last few months. You were always into acronyms, so here's one for you. I figured you'd appreciate REAL leadership. Feel free to use it with your team next year. Now, remember Coach, I wasn't an English major so if it's not grammatically correct, I'm sorry. Cut me some slack, it's my first attempt at an acronym. You can also share my cautionary tale with them and maybe it ends up becoming a great example for them. Here's what REAL leadership means to me ...

Responsible for the team
Empower others
Able to connect with others
Lead by example

RESPONSIBLE FOR THE TEAM

My whole life I've been responsible for my own success. I've worked hard and developed elite skills. If you asked me if I was responsible, I'd have always answered with a resounding 'yes'. But a real leader has a greater responsibility. It was true when I was a quarterback and it's true now as a naval aviator. I wish I had seen it all those years ago. Each team member has a responsibility to one another. But the person in charge, the person in a leadership position like I've had all my life, is especially responsible to the team.

A real leader doesn't concern themselves with the blame game. A real leader isn't so much worried about whose fault it is as they're concerned about finding solutions, moving forward, and making the best of all situations. If something goes wrong, it might not be my fault as a leader but it's certainly my responsibility to help us move forward. It might not be my fault, but it was my responsibility to help my team members. There is always something more that I can do to help my team. When I was a quarterback, I had a huge platform.

I still have a huge platform. My medals, my achievements, and my talents are noticed by many. I have a responsibility to use that power, prestige, and status for good. The SEALs like to say there are no bad teams, just bad leaders. Those guys are probably on to something. I'm blessed to have a certain level of talent and influence. Yet regrettably, my talent and my positions have been all that mattered to me.

When I had to punch out, I naturally believed that someone else had screwed up. But, as President Harry S. Truman used to say, the buck stops with me. It doesn't matter whose should get the credit or the blame. We are all in this together. A real leader is responsible for what happens on the team, not just to themselves.

EMPOWER OTHERS

Having a position of leadership has been a source of power for many years. I've loved being the captain of my teams. I've loved having men salute me here on base or an aircraft carrier. I love that I have power. But a real leader doesn't use power for their good. A real leader empowers others. I have taken care of myself my whole life. I've always worked hard to hone my skills. But I'm afraid I never really helped others to hone their skills. They were on their own. They should have a work ethic like me. They should want it as bad as I wanted it. A real leader makes other people better.

A real leader doesn't do it all by themselves but utilizes the various skillsets and value each individual brings to the team. A real leader isn't just about having compliant followers but seeks to develop other leaders. A real leader multiplies the success by spreading out the load. Everybody contributes to a team. Everyone has value. I've never taken that approach. I've never tried to catch my teammates being good. I've never been quick for praise.

Truth is that my teammates have never been able to live up to my expectations, standards, and performance. But I've also never given them a chance and I certainly never helped them to get remotely close to me. I've never really believed in the value my teammates brought to me. But we all need each other. Nobody can experience success on their own. Role players are just as valuable as the stars. We who have been stars are role players, as well. We all play a role and even though some of us might appear to have a more important role, that couldn't be further from the truth. A little $0.10 O-ring that is defective on an FA-18 can ground the whole mission. That expensive jet needs a cheap little piece of material to fly. Likewise, that little O-ring is nothing without a jet to go on. They both need each other.

It's not about me keeping my house in order and making sure I am all good. Success might be me achieving my potential and being the best I can be, but significance is when I help others be successful. A real leader empowers others so they can be the best versions of themselves.

ABLE TO CONNECT

A real leader is able to connect with all of their team members. It's not enough to have talent or be knowledgeable. It's about inspiration. A real leader can inspire the people around them. The best leaders can take someone from where they are to where they need to be. They can take people where they want to go. None of that happens if they don't trust the person. None of that happens if there is no mutual respect.

A real leader should strive to be a person of influence. No trust, no respect, no healthy communication, no encouraging words, then good luck positively influencing people. People need to believe in me as a leader and that I can help them achieve their goals, hopes, and dreams. I think everyone believed in me as a quarterback. That is, believed that I had the skills to make all the throws or the athletic ability to get out of trouble. But I wonder if people believed in me as a leader. Probably not. I didn't exactly care about my teammates. It was all about me. There was no mutual trust or respect because I didn't believe they'd ever match my abilities, work ethic, or commitment.

When I got on a receiver dropping a pass, it wasn't because the team would suffer, it was because he just hurt my stat line. Did they ever really have my back? Did they ever really do everything they could for the team I led? I don't know, but I do know that I never gave them a good reason to. I never encouraged them or connected with them on a level that would make them want to go the extra mile.

THE CAPTAIN

People don't care how much you know or how good you are if you don't care about them. It isn't a talented team that wins but rather an inspired team with talent that wins. I am not sure I ever did anything to really inspire the people around me. Real leaders connect with team members. They care about team members.

LEAD BY EXAMPLE

Real leaders set the standard and provide an example. They lead by example. I had always lived by the idea that I was leading by example. I was doing what I was supposed to do. If a teammate didn't follow my example, then it was on them. It was their problem. It was their fault. I worked hard. I studied hard. I was committed. In my mind, this was leading by example.

However, these actions were only part of the equation. I was leading by example in some other ways that I wasn't realizing. These examples were not positive. I expected my teammates to be unselfish and think about the team, but I only thought of myself. Since I was in a position of leadership, I thought that others should serve me. Though I might have been talented, I wasn't a king. I wasn't someone that people should bow down to. They were my teammates. We were all in this together.

People are always watching. They might have seen how hard I worked but they also saw that I didn't care about anyone else but myself. I was working hard and trying to be great for my benefit, not the team's benefit. I was a know-it-all. I wasn't coachable. I was the star and didn't need a coach to tell me anything. None of my coaches had won a Heisman, what could they tell me? I wasn't willing to learn or listen to anyone else. Sometimes when you're inside the frame, you can't see the picture. I needed help seeing the whole picture. I needed help seeing the whole forest and not just my tree. This attitude also rubbed off on my teammates. They wanted some of the special treatment I got. If I was leading by example and I was expecting special treatment, then it made sense they would also want special treatment. A real leader doesn't ask others to do something they're not willing to do.

If I had been a real leader, I wouldn't have expected to be served hand over foot but rather would have found ways to provide an example to others of how to be a good teammate. Great teams have great teammates. My teams at State were never great. Probably because we didn't have great teammates. This is most likely because their leader – me – never provided a good example of how to be a good teammate. I wasn't a real leader. I didn't provide the example that was most important to our team. I didn't show the way. I didn't set the example. I wasn't a servant leader. I wasn't a good teammate.

REAL LEADERS

Coach, I'm sorry I wasn't a better leader for you. I've made a lot of mistakes through the years. I can't undo them, but I look forward to leading differently moving forward. I've always had a title. I've always had a position. I've always had power. I've always had talent. I've always had status.

But what I was lacking was an understanding of what REAL leadership was all about. Despite all my achievements and leadership positions through the years, I now understand what it means to be a REAL leader.

Real leadership is about making things better. It's about making the team better. It isn't about me. It's about others.

Real leadership is about inspiring everyone to be their best.

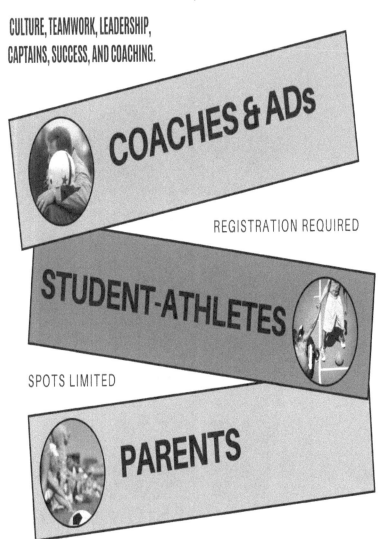

SUCCESS IS A CHOICE
WHAT CHOICE WILL YOU MAKE TODAY?

Interested in Jamy speaking at your event, working with your team, or conducting a workshop for your organization? You can connect with him at . . .

Linkedin: JamyBechler
Twitter: @CoachBechler
Website: JamyBechler.com
Instagram: @CoachBechler
Facebook: JamyBechlerLeadership
Email: speaking@JamyBechler.com

Join the 1000's of athletes, coaches, and administrators improving their leadership skills with TheLeadershipPlaybook.com. **Use coupon code "Captain" to receive a 25% discount on your membership.**

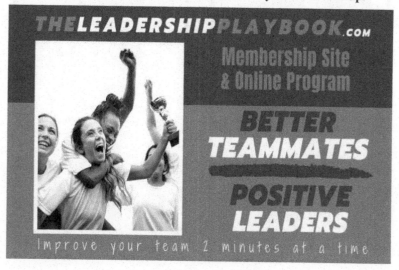

Other Books from Jamy Bechler

www.JamyBechler.com/Resources

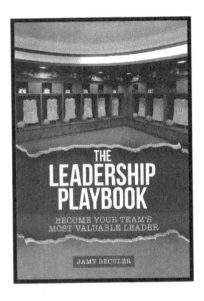

SUCCESS
is a
hosted by Jamy Bechler
CHOICE

SuccessIsAChoicePodcast.com

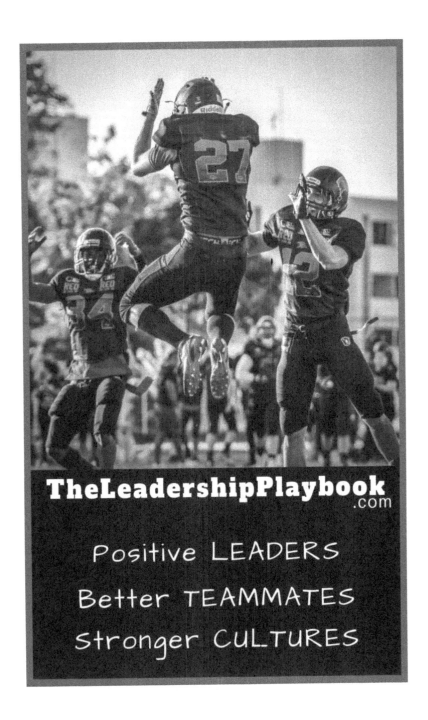